Virginia Colonial Abstracts
Vol. #15

King & Queen County, VA.
Miscellaneous Colonial & Revolutionary Records & Papers

Abstracted by:
Beverly Fleet

Southern Historical Press, Inc.

This volume was reproduced from
an 1942 edition located in the
publisher's private library,
Greenville, South Carolina

Please Direct all Correspondence & Orders to:

Southern Historical Press, Inc.
P.O. Box 1267
375 West Broad Street
Greenville, S.C. 29602-1267

Originally published: Richmond, VA., 1942
Reprinted & Retyped: Southern Historical Press, Inc.
Greenville, S.C., 2002
ISBN # 0-89308-373-9
Printed in the United States of America

PREFACE

    This, the 6th collection of King and Queen items. My readers' patience with prefaces, no doubt, has given out, as well as my own.

                                        Considerately yours,

                                              Beverley Fleet

June 30, 1942.

SUBJECT INDEX

Thomas Walker. Explorations 1750	1
George Washington Manuscrpits. Colonial Service from King and Queen. 1756-1758	2
Revolutionary Soldiers. Pension List. 1787	9
Petition of William Frazer. 1777 Warehouses for War Vessels	9
Petition of John Frayser, Jr. 1787 Re. Building Ships of War.	10
William Peachy's Certificate for George Mitchell. 1786	11
Petition of Major Thomas Armistead. 1804	12
Certificate of Major J. Pryor	12
Certificate of George Pickett, Esq.	14
Certifiacte of William Langborn for General Lafayette	15
Certificate of Hon. John Page	15
Claim of Mrs. Katherine Eubank, aged 80 years, of Monroe County, Tennessee. 1845	16

Petition of Alexander Shackleford, a Revolutionary Soldier,
    1826. Death of Griffin Fauntleroy, aide to General
    Washington at Battle of Monmouth, etc.
	19

Rejected Pension Applications. Abstracts prepared by Mrs. Eugene L. Culver.	20
Thomas Dew	21
Christopher Williams	22
William and Sarah Elliott	24
James Kelly	28
James Shepherd	30
Robert Brumfield	35

Loyalist Claims
    The Memorial of Mr. Richard Corbin, Jr. late of
        Virginia
	39

Memorial of William Graham, Attorney	43
The Memorial of Mrs. Ariana Randolph	44
The Memorial of the Rev. Samuel Henley late Professor of Moral Philosophy, etc.	45
Thomas Webb to Mrs. Mary Webb. 1783	46
Petition of the Pemunkey Indians. 1786	48
Items from Virginia Treasuary Receipts. 1770-1778	50
Petition of Wilson Lumpkin, Revolutionary Soldier. 1827	54
The Glebe Cemetary Inscriptions.	55
Spencer Roane to Governor Patrick Henry. 1786	56

Subject Index (continued)

Militia. 1793-1799   57

Capt. Richard Corbin's Artillery Company. 1812.   62

Capt. Thomas Faulkner's Company. 1812.   64

Legal Papers.

    Hill to Tompkins and Hill   68
    Wainewright vs Hill   71
    Beverley to Noel   73
    Webb to Beverley   75
    King and Queen Fees. 1794   76
    Will of Elizabeth Pendleton   77
    Campbell Notes   78
    Clayton Notes   79
    Courtney Inscriptions in Hollywood   80
    Craig's Judgement   81
    Will of Thacker Muire   82
    Beverley to Elliott   85
    Justices. 1799-1801 (Attendance at Court)   86
    Robinson to Churchill   94
    Scott to Webb Accounts for Collection   95
    Segar vs Samuel   96
    Sadler to Webb   97
    Mann vs Harwood, Jr.   98
    Dunlop and Henderson to Dunlop and Pendleton   99
    James Webb's Expense to Williamsburg   100
    Nomination of Sheriff. 1802   100
    Warehouse Inspectors. 1802   101

Thomas Walker
1750

Note: Thomas Walker, the explorer, was said to have been, physically a very powerful man. When disorders broke out in the troops, those personal fights and such, that his mere appearance quieted down everything immediately. Hence the expression that such and such a bold fellow was "Not afraid of the Devil or Tom Walker".
B.F.

Great Britain. Public Record Office, London.
Colonial Office 5. Vol. 1327. page 372.

In a letter dated May the 8th 1751, written by JOSHUA FRY to the HON. LEWIS BURWELL Esquire, President of his Majesty's Council, etc., and in turn sent by him to the Lords Commissioners of Trade and Plantations, there is a lengthy account of conditions in the frontier country. This letter includes:

"MR THOMAS WALKER on behalf of himself and a Company of other Gentlemen, who have a Grant of Land on the Waters of Mississippi, went last Year with five men to discover the Country, and look for fit Places for Settlements. He was out some months, discovered and named several of the Rivers westward of the Allegany Ridge: and built an House on Cumberland River, as is noted in the map; but he saw neither Indian or white man beyond our own settlements, which is a further Proof that the Country is not inhabited"

x x x

"MR THOMAS WALKER beforementioned went westward till he came into a flat Country, and could discover no more mountains that way; and the men who went with JOHN HOWARD say that they saw on the Mississippi and it's large Branches more good Land, than they judge is in all the English Colonies as far as they are inhabited".

Note: "Locust Grove" the home of the Walker family and birthplace of Thomas Walker, just below Walkerton in King and Queen County, is a very lovely, quiet old place. The remains of the Indian fort are still to be seen, and beyond the cemetary where members of the family rest in eternal silence, There are few monuments left. I have never seen such long graves, twelve or fifteen feet in some instances.
B.F.

COL. GEORGE WASHINGTON
Manuscripts
circa 1756

Library of Congress, Washington, D.C.
Rosters and Returns of Colonial Units from the Washington Manuscripts.
Photostats in the Virginia State Library, Richmond.

Note: It is a little difficult for me to make the reference clear in these papers. However I will do the best I can. The originals are available for those who care to see them.   B.F.

page 49. A Size Roll of MAJ'R ANDRW. LEWIS Comp'y. No date but 1755 plus and 1757 plus.
Includes:

No. 40. WILL'M FABOUS
Age 25
Size 5 ft. 7 1/2 in
Trade Planter
Country Scotland
Where Entertained, King and Queen Co.
Complection Fair
Remarks, Lusty and Good Limbs Read Hair

page 52. A Size Roll of the Seventh Company of the Virginia Regiment Commanded by CAPT. JOSH'A LEWIS. No date but 1755 plus and 1757 plus.
Includes:

No. 35. THOS DELANY
Age 40
Size 5 ft. 5 in
Trade Labourer
Country Virginia
Where entertained King and Queen
Remarks Complextion Dark

Ibid. page 52.
No. 52. WM JESSEE
Age 20
Size 5 ft. 7 in
Trade Planter
Country Virginia
Where entertained King and Queen
Complextion and Remarks Fair

(continued)

Washington Manuscripts   (continued)

Ibid. page 53.
No. 68. BENJ WILSON
Age 30
Size 5 ft 10 in
Trade Planter
Country Virginia
Where Entertained King and Queen
Complextion and Remarks   Dark

page 53.
No. 71. RICH'D BALDOCK   (about 1757)
Age 20
Size 5 ft 6
Trade Planter
Country Virginia
Where Entertained King and Queen
Complextion and Remarks   Fair

Ibid. page 54.
Size Roll of CAPT. THO'S WAGGENERs Company, at Fort Hollond on the South Branch

No. 21. JAMES WILLIMORE
County King and Queen
Age 18
Size 5 - 7
Complextion Brown
Country Virginia
Trade Planter

No. 28. JAMES FRAZIER
County King and Queen
Age 24
Size 5 - 6
Complextion Yellow
Country Scotland
Trade Planter

No. 45. JNO MAJOR
County King and Queen
Age 41
Size 5-7 1/4
Complextion Brown
Country Virginia
Trade Planter

(continued)

Washington Manuscripts (continued)

Ibid. No date but about 1757. Perhaps exactly that.
A size Roll of CAPTAIN ROBERT McKENZIEs Company.

No. 56. JOHN KEMP
Age 37
Size 5. 9 1/2
County where Enlisted King and Queen
Country Virginia
Trade -
Complexion and Remarks   Swarthy complexion. light Hair Freckled
                         well made

No. 58. JOHN EVANS
Age 30
Size 5.9
County where Enlisted King and Queen
Country Virginia
Trade -
Remarks Dark Complexion, brown hair well made

No. 59. RICH'D RIDDLE
Age 30
Size 5.6
County where Enlisted King and Queen
Remarks Dark Complexion brown hair well made

page 62. A Necessary Role of CAPT WAGGONER's Company
JAMES WILLMORE's equipment was: (no date)
JAMES FRASER equipment was

Fire Lock	1	Knapsack	1
Bayonett	1	Blanket	1
Cartridge Box	1	Comb	1
Cartredges	12	Canteen	0
Belt and frog	1	Sword	0
Coate	1	Shash	0
Westcoate	1		
Britches	1		
Hat	1		
Cockade	1		
Shirts	3		
Stocks	2		
Stockings	2		
Shoes	1		
Shoe Buckels	1		
Knee Buckels	1		
Garter and buckels	1		
Haversack	1		

Note: No sash, no sword, but little did these young ruffians
realize the veneration this equipment would be regarded. A
most indifferent bit of metal, wrapped in brocade and marked
"My father's knee buckle" has survived these many years. B.F.

Washington Manuscripts (continued)

Ibid. page 102.
A Size Roll of LIEUT: COL'O: STEPHEN's Company July the 13th 1756
Includes:

No. 14. KILLIS COLLIS
When enlisted May 25 1755
Where enlisted King and Queen
Age 18
Size f ft 6 in
Trade Planter
Country Virginia
Description Brown Hair, well made

No. 16. RICHARD BALDACK
Where enlisted Essex
Age 19
Size 5 ft 5 in
Trade Planter
Country Virginia
Description Light Hair fair complexion well made

No. 17. GOWEN BEAZELEY
When enlisted May 1st 1756
Where enlisted Caroline
Age 20
Size 5 ft 7 in
Trade Carpenter
Country Virginia
Description Dark Hair brown Complexion   very handsome

No. 21. JOHN PERRY
When enlisted 1755
Where enlisted Caroline County
Age 31
Size 5 ft 3 in
Trade Cordwainer
Country Wales
Description Brown Complexion

No. 27. JOHN COLE
When enlisted May 5th 1756
Where enlisted Caroline
Age 30
Size 5 ft 8 in
Trade Planter
Country Virginia
Description Black Bushy Hair a very thick Beard Spare made

Washington Manuscripts (continued)

Ibid. page 104. A Roll of CAPT CHARLES LEWIS's Company. July 13th 1756
Includes:

No. 3. JAMES CARSON
Enlisted when   1754 March
Enlisted where King and Queen
Age 24
Size 5 ft 9 in
Trade Bricklayer
Country English
Description Brown with Black Hair

No. 6. THOS EDMONDSON
Enlisted when   1755 Sep'r
Enlisted where Essex
Age 25
Size 5 ft 8 in
Trade Planter
Country Virginian
Description Fair and Sandy Hair

No. 27. FRANCIS THOMAS
Enlisted when   Draft May
Enlisted where King William
Age 18
Size 5 ft 7 in
Trade Planter
Country Virginian
Description Brown dark Hair. well limbed

No. 4. SAMPSON FRANKLIN
Enlisted when   1755 Septr
Enlisted where Caroline
Age 20
Size 5 ft 5 in
Trade Planter
Country Virginian
Description Brown and brown Hair

page 116. A Roll of CAP'T THOMAS COCKE's Company July 13th 1756
Includes:

No 12. THOMAS EDWARDS   When Enlisted Decem'r 25, 1755
Where Enlisted King William   Age 27   Size 5 ft 5 in
Trade Taylor   Country Wales
Description   Black Hair   Yellow Complexion and wanting the
                            left Eye

Washington Manuscripts (continued)

Ibid. page 124.
A Size Roll of CAPT THOMAS WAGGENERs Company September 19th 1756
Includes:

JAMES WILLMORE
Height feet 5
      Inches 7
Age 18
Complection Brown
Countrey Virginia
Trade Planter
From where draught King and Queen
Description Straight dark hair. Wellmade and full smooth face

JOHN REA
Height feet 5
      Inches 10
Age 22
Complection Fair
Country Virginia
Trade Blacksmith
From where draught King William
Description Spare made long neck a little head and smooth face.

Ibid. page 143. A Muster Roll of CAPT ROBERT STEWARTs Company In the Virginia Regiment. August 1st 1757.
Includes:

No. 40. JAMES CHICK
Age 23
Size 5 ft 9 1/2 in
By whom Inlisted By Act of Assembly
When Inlisted Oct 15, 1756
Country Virginia
Trade Sadler
Where Entertained Winchester
County Inlisted King and Queen
Particular Description Ruddy Complextion thin long nose
                            short brown hair

page 145. A Size Roll of COLLO WASHINGTONs Company August 28th 1757
Includes:

No. 4. JNO TRIGG
When Inlisted Nov'r 1754 County King and Queen Age 25
Size 5 Feet 7 1/2 inches Trade Planter Country Virginia
Description Brown Complextion and hair, well Set

Washington Manuscripts   (continued)

page 156. Size Roll of CAP'T WOODARDs Company Sept'r the - (24th?)   1757.
Includes:

JOHN SORRELL
Where Born   Virginia
Age 35
Size 5.9
County   King and Queen   Complection Brown   Trade   Planter
Remarks   Black Hair and foolish speech

Note: Once, far from here and long ago, I was on a journey. There were two endless nights and no such thing as sleep. A man, who told me his name was Sorrell and that he was from Virginia came and sat with me. Never have I had a more delightful companion, or one who could more aptly turn drab dull things into comedy. Now was this foolish speech? If so, I am fool enough to think not.   B.F.

page 160. There is a slip or two in modern spelling here. Let's have it.
"A Size Rool of CAPT ROB'T SPOTSWOODs Company Fort Young Octob'r the 7: 1757"
Includes:

No. 44. JOHN GUTHRY
Age   31
Size   feet 5
       inches 9
Trade   planter
Country   Virginia
Whear Enlisted   King and Queen
Complection Fair
Remarks Well made and Light Coloured Hair

page 162. A Return for the month of Septr 1757 of the Virginia Regiment Commanded by GEORGE WASHINGTON Esqr Fort Loudoun Octr 1. 1757
Companies   COL'O WASHINGTONs   CAPT LEWIS
            MAJOR LEWIS   CAPT WOODWARDs
            CAPT WAGGENNERs   CAPT SPOTSWOODs
            CAPT STEWARTs   CAPT McKENZIEs
                     Draughts not Companies

page 178. "A list of the mens Names Belonging to the 1st Virginia Regiment that was kild in last Action near Fort du Quesne Sept'r 14th 1758". 8 officers, one of whom, MAJOR LEWIS is listed as a prisoner, and 59 men killed. The names are illegible.

8

Washington Manuscripts (continued)

page 194. No date, but 1756 according to other lists in the group.

A List of the soldiers Inlisted in King and Queen County

	Age	where born	Complexion	Trade	size ft.	in.
JOHN EVANS	26	Virginian	Fair	Planter	5	10
JOHN COLE	30	Do	Black	Do	5	9
RICHARD BALDOCK	19	Do	Fair	Do	5	5
ACHILLIS COLLINS	18	Do	Do	Do	5	5 1/2
JAMES WILLMORE	18	Do	Brown	Do	5	6
THOMAS GREGORY	18	Do	Fair	Do	5	11
WILLIAM BARTON	19	Do	Do	Carpenter	6	
FRANCIS SAUNDERS	20	Do	Dark	Taylor	5	4
JOHN KENYHAM	20	Do	Do	Planter	5	8

* * * * * * *

REVOLUTIONARY SOLDIERS

Commonwealth of Virginia
Auditor's Office
Pension List 1787

Includes:

BANKS DUDLEY. Age 35. Serjeant 7th Virginia Regt. Ł 18.
BENJAMIN HOOMES, King and Queen County. Captain 2d Va. Regt.
    Ł 144
COSBY FOSTER. Age 20. Private. 3rd Regt. dragoons. Ł 15

* * * * * * *

PETITION OF WILLIAM FRAZER

Archives Division. Virginia State Library, Richmond.
King William County Petitions. Nov. 17th 1777.

To the Honourable the Speaker and Gentlemen of the House of Delegates
The humble Petition of WILLIAM FRAZER, sheweth
    That your Petitioner conceives the Warehouses in King William County, called Quarles's are very improperly placed, both to the public convenience and for Vessels receiving Tobacco from thence, as

The Petition of WILLIAM FRAZER   (continued)

they are situated at least Half a Mile from the River, and the
Road leading to them occasions a Road to run through the Middle
of a Tract of Land, late the Property of ROBERT NELSON, Esq'r
but now the Property of your Petitioner, and which is much
injured thereby

    Your Petitioner lives about a Mile below these Warehouses,
and keeps a ferry, well known to many of your Honourable House:
and having a fine Wharf and Landing for Vessels, and a very
convenient Place for a Warehouse, he proposes, in Behalf of
himself, to remove the Warehouses to his Landing, and there
erect them, as convenient for the Public as he can; and in
future to keep them up at his own Expence, whereby these Advantages will arise to the Public, that the Warehouses will be
fixed at a more convenient Place for the People, fna for the
Shippers of Tobacco.

    Your Petitioner will thereby be able to store the Rigging
and Sails of the public armed Vessels, when and where they come
to heave down and refit; and in future no Expense shall arise
to the Public from keeping up the said Warehouses; all which
Advantages your Petitioner hopes will be sufficient to induce
your Honourable House to grant the prayer of this Petition; and,
as in Duty bound, will ever pray

Endorsed: "WILL FRAZER
                      Nov. 17th 1777
                     Ref'd to Prop'ns
                 Ref'd to Consideration next
                     Session of Assembly
                         Reasonable"

* * * * * *

THE PETITION OF JOHN FRAYSER, JR.
1787

Archives Division. Virginia State Library, Richmond
King William Co. Petitions. 22 Nov. 1787
Marked "Rejected".

    To the Honourable the Speaker and Members of the House of
General Assembly the Petition of JOHN FRAYSER Jun'r, Executor
and son to WILLIAM FRAYSER deceased, late of King William
County humbly sheweth, that your Petitioners Father was employed
by the Navy board in the year 1776 Jointly with MR JOHN ROANE
to furnish supplies to the Builders and necessaries for the
Ships of War then Building on Matopony River, that the said
WILLIAM FRAYSER and JOHN ROANE acted

Petition of JOHN FRAYSER, Jr. (continued)

as Agents untill sometime in 1777 when Mr Roane declined acting any longer, the whole business devolved on WILLIAM FRAYSER, who it is well known from his attachment to his Country and his implicit confidence in the Navy Board and the Governing Powers, advanced and became answerable to sundry Persons for very considerable sums of money. That your Petitioner since the death of his Father, has been sued for a very large sum his Fathers engagement to pay on account of the said Agency, in so much that his Estate has been mostly sold and is insufficient to pay the many demands, against it. Your Petitioner has Exhibited a State of his Fathers Accompt to the Auditors and has requested a settlement. This the auditor has appeared willing to make, but insists on paying your Petitioner the balance appearing due to him by the Depretiation of 1779, because this was a time when the last sum was advanced to your Petitioners Father. Whereas it appears, a good deal of the money was advanced for the State in 1776, some in 1777 and 1778 and 1779.

By the mode of settlement proposed by the Auditor Your Petitioner will get little or nothing for the large sums he advanced for the Commonwealth. Your Petitioner is willing to adjust the whole Account of debit and Credits, by the scale of depreciation, which he conceives to be the Just and legal way and not to bring the early advances in 1777 and 1778 to be scaled by the depreciation of 1779 mearly (sic) because your Petitioners Father was obliged to accept at that time a partial payment. Your Petitioner conceives this mode so unjust, that he cannot in Justice to himself and his Fathers Family submit to it, untill compelled by a refusal to redress, what he conceaves to be a real Grievance.

Your Petitioner therefore prays your Honourable House, to take the same in to your consideration and allow him such relief as the Justice of his case requires, and to direct a payment to him, in such certificates or warrants, as will answer Your Petitioners purpose in paying the Debts of his Father - and as in duty bound he will ever pry &c

* * * * *

COL. WM. PEACHEY's CERTIFICATE FOR
GEORGE MITCHELL

Official Papers. Virginia State Library, Richmond
Patrick Henry, April 1786

Richmond County Sc
GEORGE MITCHELL made oath before me WILLIAM PEACHEY one of the Magistrates of the said county that he served in the continental Line of this state, to the southward, untill the second Day of November 1782 when he received a written discharge from CAPT BEVERLY ROY, which has been since lost or mislaid, for which service he never re-

Col. Peachey's Certificate for George Mitchell (continued)

ceived any pay, or Wages, and only the following articles of Cloathing Viz 2 hats, one shirt, one pr overalls, four pr shoes and one black stock or neckcloth:
Given under my hand this 14th Day of April 1784

WILL: PEACHEY

Endorsed: WM PEACHEYs Certif
for G MITCHELL

Note: Let us hope that none of our modern war profiteers (or some of our warriors) will ever see the Petition of JOHN FRAYSER, Jr., or Mitchell's certificate. It might hurt their feelings.   B.F.

* * * * * *

THE PETITION OF MAJOR THOMAS ARMISTEAD

Archives Division. Virginia State Library, Richmond
King and Queen County Petitions. 19 Dec. 1804

To the honorable, the general assembly of the commonwealth of Virginia
The petition of THOMAS ARMISTEAD humbly sheweth
That your petitioner, in the month of May, in the year 1775, was appointed ensign of a company of volunteers in the county of King and Queen, commanded by CAPT. GEORGE LYNE: that his company, being united, by the order of the committee of safety, with a company of minutemen, was in service at Hampton in September 1775, when it was attacked by the British: that your petitioner afterwards did duty, as a volunteer in the 7th Virginia regiment, in the company of CAPT GREGORY SMITH, at the time of the declaration of independence: that in the same year your petitioner was appointed third lieutenant of marines and performed garrison duty with the said regiment in York Town: that your petitioner was then turned over to the first Virginia State regiment, commanded by COL'O GEORGE GIBSON: which regiment in the year 1777 was attached to GENERAL MUHLENGURG's brigade in the continental army; that the enlistment of men having expired in the winter of 1780, your petitioner returned to Virginia to recruit: that from the frequent invasion of this country your petitioner was detailed by express orders from various services of an active and exposed kind, until the siege of York, when your petitioner became a member of Dabney's legion: that your petitioner (was) afterward ordered to garrison Portsmouth, and was then permitted to retire, but under the Special order of Executive, that he should be continued in service

Notwithstanding the facts, contained in the foregoing representation: - facts, which can now be proved by many patriots of these days,

The Petition of Major Thos. Armistead (continued)

yet living: - your petitioner is among the few, who have not received the emoluments allowed to the army in general. He pretends not to boast of merit; but he dares to appeal to any test for the truth, and nature of his exertions in the cause of independence.

Why your petitioner has not applied at an earlier day for the compensation, conferred on others, he can assign no better reason, than an inattention to his pecuniary affairs, in which he cannot now persevere without essential injury to his family.

Your petitioner therefore prays, that he will be indulged in his rights, which have been earned with personal hazard, and if they are forfeited, have been forfeited by no dishonor.

THOS. ARMISTEAD

The Auditor has no knowledge of the circumstances stated in the petitioner therefore cannot say anything on the subject.

S: SHEPARD

Endorsed: Armistead's pet'o
                         to
                      Claims
            refer'd 19 Dec 1804

Further endorsed: Petition of THOMAS
                    ARMISTEAD
                    Reasonable
                    Jan 1 1805

Certificate attached to foregoing paper:

I do hereby Certify that during the Campaigns of 1778 and 1779 whilst acting as Aide Camp to MAJR. GEN'L. LORD STIRLING, I became acquainted with CAPT. THOS. ARMISTEAD then of the first Virg's State Regt. in Continental Service and I have a perfect recollection that his zeal for the American Cause and promptitude for command on any Enterprize or Expedition of Emergency were frequently Evinced and that he was considered as a brave and active officer by all who were acquainted with him.

Richmond January 4th 1805

J. PRYOR

Other papers attached to Major Armisteads petition.

I feel a pleasure in stating that the conduct of CAPT. THOMAS ARMISTEAD, whilst he resided near Norfolk, was, as far as ever came within my knowledge, such as became a sound and inflexible republican

DANIEL BEDINGER

Richmond Jan'y 8th 1804

The Petition of Major Thos. Armistead (continued)

Other papers attached to the petition.

This is to certify that some time, probably in the fall, of the year 1781, I conducted a number of Deserters, eighteen and six months men from Hampshire Jail to Winchester and delivered them to a certain Colonel Green. I also certify that I frequently understood about that time that a Major Armistead was a receiving Officer of the above description of men for the Army
Given under my hand at Richmond this 8th day of January 1805
Test
SAML COLEMAN   JOHN PRUNTY

CERTIFICATE OF GEORGE PICKETT ESQ

    In the Summer 1781 there was a Report that GENERAL ARNOLD with a large force of British Soldiers were coming to Richmond in consequence of which all the vessells that Lay at and below Rockets fell down the River to a place called Cox & dale: there they met General Arnold the Enemy commenced a fire with cannon on our vessells from the south side, and in a very little time they took possession of one of our armed vessells, and turned the cannon on the Remainder of our vessells - at this time the Commanding officer (COL'O INNES) ordered Major Armistead with all the Troops under his Command to go to the Waters Edge and to defend the vessells to the last Extremity. Major Armistead did take his post on the water Edge and as near the vessells as he could get and continued there from about ten oclock in the forenoon till dark - he was Exposed to the Enemy fire the whole day - and kept up a Continual fire on the Enemy - near night COL'O TURNER SOUTHALL came to me and said it was COL'O INNES orders that Major Armistead should Bring his men of the Ground and desired me to go to him with these orders - this I did and found Major Armistead Exposed very much to the Enemys fire, and was told that several of his men were killed and wounded.
    I told Major Armistead that it was the Commanding officers orders that he should Bring his men of the ground as there was little or no chance to save the vessells - they at that time being abandoned by the Capts and Saylors. Major Armistead answer was that he had hopes of saving sum of the vessells that lay nearest the shore, he continued thru untill I came away and left him there
    Given under my hand this third day of Jan'y 1805

                                                   GEO PICKETT

Endorsed: GEORGE PICKETT Esqr
                            Certificate
                         Jan 3d 1805.

The Petition of MAJOR THOS. ARMISTEAD (continued)

Other papers attached to the petition.

          King Wm. County Decm'r 30th
               1804

  I believe myself authorised in the absence of the MARQUIS DE LA FAYETTE, to declare to the Assembly and my country, the confidence and respect the Gen'l. had for the zeal, activity, and patriotism of MAJOR THOS. ARMISTEAD. To my knowledge he has often been selected for dangerous and important enterprises, and I believe the Genl's orders will certify his approbation of his gen'l conduct. For my own part I recollect with pleasure the services that Maj. Armistead rendered his country, and shall be gratified if this certificate should procure for him what the Legislature in their wisdom and justice shall think just to grant him

              WM LANGBORN

Memorandum included with other papers.

         Remarks (Maj'r Pryors Certificate
  In the year 1780 COL'O GEO. GIBSONs Reg't cal'd the first State Reg't. In Continental Service returned from the North to Virg'a. the men whose time of Inlistment had expir'd were discharg'd and those enlisted for the War retired on furlow, afterwards assembled in Williamsburg and in the Summer or Spring of 1781 was stationed at Peters Burg at which places (as above) I was with the regiment. In 1781 see the order of Counsel for the orgainiseation of the State Troops in a Legion. See GEO PICKETTs Esqr Certificate, see Majr Langborns Certificate, and his Excellency's JOHN PAGE Esqr, also JOHN PRUNTY's Esqr Certificate at the seige of York, MAJOR FREDERICK WOODSONs Testimony, the State troops at Portsmouth, MAJR F. WOODSON, COL'O THOS NEWTON Esqr also pay Roll Testimony F WOODSON Esqr

The above memo in the hand-writing of whoever wrote the text of Major Thos. Armistead's petition. The hand-writing being different from his signature

Letter Addressed: MAJOR THO'S. ARMISTEAD
           Richmond

              Richmond Jan'y 3d. 1805

Dear Sir
  As my state of health, and of the weather forbids my going before the Committee, to whom your case is referred, I can only give you in writing the substance of what I could say were I to attend, as you had requested.
  And that is, that I had often heard of your bold and enterprizing spirit, and military skill, whilst I was in the Committee of safety, and council of state: and remember upon an interesting occasion,

The Petition of MAJOR THOS. ARMISTEAD (continued)

Other papers attached to the petition.

    during Arnolds Invasion, your assistance was called for by Col'l Innes, and readily afforded with ability. I mean on the night after Arnold returned from his Expedition to Richmond, and had appeared off Jamestown, and it was apprehended that he would land and endeavour to cut off the militia under Gen'l Nelson and Col Innes, which had, by a forced march, been thrown into Williamsburg, and which, being too weak (without the aid of the Militia which had been ordered down from Holts Forge, and was expected in, the next day) to make a successful resistance, and then form the junction contemplated with the reinforcements expected, were removed in the night from Williamsburg, up the road, by which the communication with the expected militia, was necessary to be kept open: I say that I remember that you formed the militia that night, and acted as a Major, and that Col. Innes mentioned to me your great military worth. But as I had not been in the Army, and could not recollect the rank, and even the names of but few of our Officers, I do not remember anything more of your Rank, than that you were called Captain, and then Major Armistead and that you were very early in the service, and that I witnessed your service at a late and interesting Period of the War.

    Major Langborn's certificate is a confirmation of what I had heard respecting you and is highly valuable, as he was a favorite Aid de Camp of the MARQUISS DE LA FAYETTE

                          I am dear Sir
                          Your obed't. Serv't.
                          JOHN PAGE

* * * * * *

CLAIM OF MRS. KATHERINE EUBANK

Land Office. Capitol Building, Richmond, Virginia
Loose Manuscripts.

State of Tennessee)
Monroe County   ) SS

    This day personally appeared before me ALEXANDER SLOAN an acting Justice of the peace in and for the county aforesaid and one of the Justices of the County Court for said County and State.
    KATHERINE EUBANK, a resident of said county and of the thirteenth civil District thereof, aged now about Eighty years, who being first duly sworn according to Law, doth on her oath depose and say that she is the widow of JOHN EUBANK, and was lawfully married to him about the year seventeen hundred and eighty four in King and Queen County, in the state of Virginia, that the marriage took place as said in the

The Claim of MRS. KATHERINE EUBANK (continued)

summer of said year: That her husband the said JOHN EUBANK Inlisted in the Army of the United States in the Virginia Continental Line about the first of the year seventeen hundred and seventy-six for three years, that after the expiration of said term he received an honorable discharge having faithfully served out the time of his enlistment, and returned home about the first of the year seventeen hundred and seventy-nine: that afterwards, to wit: about the last of the year seventeen hundred and seventy nine or the first of the year seventeen hundred and eighty, her husband, the said JOHN EUBANK, again enlisted in King and Queen county, where he resided, for during the war: that he served for about two years until after the Surrender of Cornwallis at Yorktown and was again honorably discharged: that he returned home and about the summer of seventeen and eighty-four married said deponant as aforesaid, that his before described services in the Revolutionary was as a private, in whcih capacity he had served the State of Virginia issued to him two Military Land Warrents, the evidence upon which they were issued and the evidence of the fact of their issue, she suppose to be on file in the Virginia Military Land Office, which is hereby referred to: that her husband, the said JOHN EUBANK entrusted the said Land Warrents to the care of LONY MALONE to locate them, and that the said LONY MALONE lost his said Land Warrents and the aforesaid JOHN EUBANK never received grants thereon: and that she now desires that duplicate warrents issue to her in lieu of those lost as above described

Sworn to and Subscribed before)
me this 9th day April 1845)
ALEX. SLOAN (seal))
A Justice of the Peace for said County

            her
         KATHERINE X EUBANK
            mark

State of Tennessee)
Monroe County) S.S.

  I HENRY L. KING aged now near fifty one years do hereby certify that I have been acquainted with KATHERINE EUBANK, who has sworn and subscribed the above deposition, for about thirty-five years: that I was first acquainted with her in Guilford County, North Carolina, about the time of the decease of her husband, JOHN EUBANK; that the said JOHN EUBANK died I believe in Guilford County North Carolina, and in the neighborhood in which he resided at, and before the time of his death, he was generally reported and believed to have been a revolutionary soldier, and I concur in that opinion. I then understand that the said JOHN EUBANK had received two Military Land Warrents from the State of Virginia for his services in the Revolutionary War: that he had entrusted them to the care of LONY MALONE to locate and that the said Malone had lost them, and I have always understood that the Widow, KATHERINE EUBANK and her children have never received grants on said

The Claim of MRS. KATHERINE EUBANK (continued)

warrents. And I further certify that KATHERINE EUBANK is and intilligent (sic) and credible person, a woman of the strictest truth and veracity, and I believe her to be eighty years of age, and know her to be the same person who was the reputed lawful wife, and widow of JOHN EUBANK in Guilford County, North Carolina

Sworn to and Subscribed) H. S. KING
before me this 9th day of April)
1845)
ALEX SLOAN
A Justice of the Peace &c

State of Tennessee)
Monroe County)

    I, ALEXANDER SLOAN, an acting Justice of the peace and one of the Justices of the County Court for said County and State, do hereby certify that KATHERINE EUBANK who has sworn to and subscribed the above deposition is an intilligent and credible person, that I believe her to be eighty years of age and would be unable to appear in open court to make her deposition. And I further certify that I am also well acquainted with HENRY L. KING, whose affadavit precedes this certificate who is an intilligent and credible person and a citizen of said County and State
    Given under my hand this 9th day of April 1845

                               ALEX. SLOAN (seal)
                               a Justice of the peace
                                                 &c.

These papers also include certificate of JOHN A. STEPHENS, clerk of the Court of Monroe County, Tennessee, and a certificate of JOHN CARSON, Presiding Justice of the County. Both dated 16 April 1845.

THE PETITION OF ALEXANDER SHACKELFORD
A REVOLUTIONARY SOLDIER

Archives Department, Virginia State Library, Richmond.
King and Queen County Petitions. 6 Dec. 1826

Endorsed:	The Petition of
ALEXANDER SHACKELFORD
of King & Queen
(a soldier of the Revolution)
praying to be placed on
the pension list
JNO MASON
Decr 6th 1826
ref'd to Claims
1826. Decr 23rd
Rejected
26 Reported

To the honorable The General Assembly of the State of Virginia
The petition of ALEXANDER SHACKELFORD of the county of King & Queen and state aforesaid a soldier of the revolution. Humbly sheweth That your petitioner was enlisted on the 3rd day of February 1777 by CHARLES COLLIER a capt in the first Regiment of the "Virginia line" then in Williamsburg, that on 29th March following your petitioner march'd with the company to which he belonged from Williamsburg to Valley Forge in the state of New Jersey at which place the troops arrived on the 29th of April following. That your petitioner was at the battle of Monmouth fought on the 28th June 1778 in which Battle Your petitioner had the sight of his right eye taken away by the violent wind produced by a twelve pound cannon ball passing within two inches of his face which ball directly after killed GRIFFIN FAUNTLEROY aid to GENERAL WASHINGTON by whom he was then on horse back. That from aforesaid disaster Your petitioner was confined from 28th June to 29th November 1778. Your petitioner was after his discharge from the hospital on various duties until October 1779 when he with all who took no certificate of enlistment were turned over to the Continental Establishment, after which your petitioner was at the Seige of Yorktown by General Washington which was surrendered to the American troops on the 19th of October 1781.
On the 29th October your petitioner was discharged and returned to his friends in King and Queen where he has remained ever since a peaceable cultivator of the soil for his subsistence. Your petitioner is now in the 67th year of his age. Worn out at length with labour he is no longer able to support himself by the labour of his hands.
Your petitioner Therefore prays that your honorable body will make some provision for his maintenance in his latter days and your petitioner will ever pray

ALEXANDER SHACKELFORD

(continued)

The Petition of ALEXANDER SHACKELFORD (continued)

King and Queen County towit
ALEXANDER SHACKELFORD personally appeared before me a justice of the peace for the county aforesaid and made oath that he is the same person who is described in the above petition and that he signed the same
Given under my hand this 28th day of November 1826

RO. M. SPENCER J.P.

King and Queen County to wit
MINETRY SPENCER and LAWRENCE CROUCH two Credible witnesses personally appeared before me a Justice of the peace for the County aforesaid and being duly sworn depose and say that they and each of them are well acquainted with ALEXANDER SHACKELFORD and his situation in life, and know him to be the same person described in the above petition and by reason of his great age and infirmaties to be unable to support himself by labour, and further that the said ALEXANDER SHACKELFORD is a poor man and needs assistance.
Given under my hand this 28th day of November 1826

RO. M. SPENCER, J.P.

* * * * * *

REJECTED PENSION APPLICATIONS

Note: Mrs. Florence B. Culver (Mrs. Eugene L. Culver) of the Martha Washington Chapter, D.A.R., chairman of the New Kent Records Committee, No. 5115 Forty Fifth St., N.W., Washington, D.C., has been kind and generous enough to send the following items, which she obtained in Washington. I quote from her letter of August 16th 1939. "I am enclosing abstracts of the six rejected pension applications for King and Queen and King William Counties. x x . I find there are about 160 names mentioned in these six papers. I do not know whether you like this kind of material as well as I do, or not; but it seems to me quite valuable, since it gives in so many cases birth dates, marriage and sometimes death dates of rather obscure people that it would not be otherwise possible to find out about at all. The more prominent families are often written up, or can be found in State records; therefore I feel particularly grateful for the material given us from the Pension Office. x x x and when I had an extra hour would run over to the Navy Department where the Pension records are kept and copy awhile". At the end of Mrs. Culver's notes, which follow, she remarks "Very, very sad that these poor old men were so mistreated".
We must be very grateful indeed to Mrs. Culver, who has family, club and many social obligations, for making this date available for

Rejected Pension Applications (continued)

us. It is a case of a great deal of careful work - and that work it's own and only reward. B.F.

THOMAS DEW
King and Queen Co.

Rejected Application for Revolutionary Pension
No. R 2. 909.

On 10th March 1842 appeared personally before JOHN LUMPKIN, justice of peace in said county, THOMAS DEW, of said county, aged 78 years, who declared: that in the spring of 1780 he entered the service of the U.S., under CAPT. EDMUND PENDLETON of Caroline Co., and that another Co., commanded by CAPT PHILIP JOHNSON also of Caroline Co., marched with his company from Caroline Co., through Richmond to Hillsborough, N.C. where with other troops they made a brigade commanded by GENERAL EDWARD STEVENS. HOLT RICHESON was one of the Colonels. Joined main army under GENERAL GATES at Ridgely and in August was in the engagement known as Gates Defeat. Was discharged at Guilford Court House, N.C., having been in service 6 months. He again enlisted in April 1781 under CAPT. HENRY LUMPKIN in the County of King and Queen and marched to Falmouth where Capt Lumpkin resigned, and Dew was put under Capt. Quarles, attached to Weeden (Wheeden) brigade, marched to Fulvanna Co., and joined La Fayette and Wayne and marched to a place near Williamsburg and back to Malvin Hills, below Richmond, where "my month expiring I was discharged".

Judge Lumpkin states that THOMAS DEW, Esq., is a gentleman of the highest standing, of unimpeachable veracity, etc., and that because he (Dew) is of advanced age and lives a great distance from the court house - he pleads for proper consideration of his application, as it is difficult for him to get to and attend Court.

Another paper says: At Quarterly Court of King and Queen County, Monday 14th March 1842, the proceedings of JOHN LUMPKIN's court in relation to THOMAS DEW's application is certified to the War Dep't.

Signed by ROBERT POLLARD, JR.,
Clerk of Court.

A letter attached to application says: that Mr Dew is now worth about $200.000. And that he wants the pension allowance for some charitable purpose. "Mr Dew is the father of the President of William and Mary College, Va. and in point of standing as a gentleman of veracity has no superior". "He does not recollect a man who was with him in service now living. He recollected a Mr. Long, but he is dead", etc.

signed by FRANCIS V. SUTTON
Bowling Green, Va.
Dated 17 Sept. 1842.   Caroline Co.

Rejected Pension Applications   (continued)

Application of THOMAS DEW.
A letter from Pension Office. Addressed to FRANCIS V. SUTTON, Esq., of Bowling Green, dated 22 Sept. 1842. (in abstract) says that the claim is unsupported and full of errors. The first term of service was known to be 3 months and not 6, and since the 2nd term of service was admitted to be but 1 month, the applicant had not served 6 mos. in all, which is sufficient to defeat his claim to a pension.
No signature.

End of THOMAS DEW's papers

Note: To save my soul I cannot throw myself into an agony of sympathy at this refusal. $200.00. was a right fat fortune way down yonder at that period.
    Malvin Hills is of course Malvern Hill an estate belonging to the Cocke family.   B.F.

* * * * * *

CHRISTOPHER WILLIAMS
King and Queen Co.

Rejected Application.
No. R 11.564

On 13 April 1835, in open Court of King and Queen County, CHRISTOPHER WILLIAMS aged 72 years, declared (under oath) that he enlisted in the army of U.S. in October 1781, with CAPT CHRISTOPHER RONE for the war, and did serve in Capt. Rone's company of artillery of the State Establishment until the close of the war in 1783, as the following statement shows:
    From Oct. 1781 to Nov. 1783 (2 years) under Lieut. Harper, Capt. Rone and Col. Harrison. His place of abode was King and Queen County, Virginia. Vouched for by A. SHACKLEFORD, GEORGE GOODMAN and POLLY WATTS.
    Was stationed at Yorktown remaining until Nov. 1783. Then was marched to Richmond where rec'd regular discharge from Capt. Rone (which he lost). After the surrender of "Wallace" there were no other troops left at Yorktown but Capt Rone's Co. of artillery, which was turned over to the Continental Establishment. Etc.

                                               his
                    Signed   CHRISTOPHER X WILLIAMS
                                               mark

MR. JOHN SUMMERSON, a clergyman in the county of King and Queen, and WILLIAM MORRIS residing in the same, do hereby certify that they are well acquainted with CHRISTOPHER WILLIAMS, believe him to be 72 years

Rejected Pension Applications   (continued)

CHRISTOPHER WILLIAMS

old and that he is generally believed to be a soldier of the Revolution.

A questionaire attached says - Williams was born in 1763. He lived at time of entering service in King and Queen and still lives there. Says he Enlisted in the service. That he knows in his neighborhood MR. WILLIAM MORRIS, CAPT. ROBT. BLAND and many others who can testify to his veracity and that he served in the Revolution.
ROBERT POLLARD, JR., Clark of the Court, certifies the papers. April 1835.

On another paper, ALEXANDER SHACKLEFORD, a Revolutionary Soldier, aged 75 yrs on 27th of next October (1834) of King and Queen Co. That he is well acquainted with the applicant CHRISTOPHER WILLIAMS and knows him to have been a soldier of the Revolution in Company of Capt. Rone from Oct. 1781 to end of the war.
Dated 12 May 1834. Sworn to before THOMAS F. SPENCER, J.P.

MRS. POLLY WATTS of Middlesex County gives affidavit 27th day of Nov. 1834, that she knows Williams and is sure he was a regular soldier of the Revolution. Sworn before PHILIP T. MONTAGUE, J.P.

GEORGE GARDINER, a revolutionary soldier, aged 75, of County of Middlesex, also states Williams surely served in the Revolution, etc.
Sworn before PHILIP T. MONTAGUE, J.P. GEORGE HEALY, Clerk of Middlesex Co., also signed.

JOHN RICHARDS of King and Queen County, as agent for CHRISTOPHER WILLIAMS, sends a letter to J.L. EDWARDS, Esq., Com. of Pensions, with additional evidence and the papers, asking that when acted upon, the pension certificate be directed to "Mr Bowlers" post office.

Affidavit of CARTER CROXTON, a revolutionary soldier, aged 74 years, of Essex County, is attached. Sworn before PETER J. DERIEUX, J.P.

A warrant for 200 acres of land for CHRISTOPHER WILLIAMS, dated 26th April 1783, signed by BENJ. HARRISON and THOS. MERIWETHER, is copied from the Land Office of Virginia and filed with these papers.

ROBERT BLAND certifies that he is well acquainted with CHRISTOPHER WILLIAMS and was raised in the same neighborhood, believes him to be truthful, etc. June 1835.

FRANCIS ROW states that he has known "old MR. CHRISTOPHER WILLIAMS" for at least 30 years and believes him truthful.
11 June 1835

THOS. F. SPENCER and GAVIN UPSHAW of King and Queen send signed

Rejected Pension Applications   (continued)

CHRISTOPHER WILLIAMS.

affidavits that they know CHRIS WILLIAMS 'of this county', and have known him for 25 or 30 years and think him truthful. 11 June 1835.

A letter dated 6 May 1835 and headed "BOWLERS P.O." encloses what Williams claims is his discharge, which he has found. Footnote initialed R.E. states that they agree that the discharge is "spurious", and that the date "Nov 1783" is absurd. The spelling of the Capt's name Rone ridiculous and the marking of the paper obvious.

     End of CHRISTOPHER WILLIAMs' Papers.

      * * * * * * *

WILLIAM ELLIOTT
SARAH ELLIOTT

Rejected Application.
No. R 3.307

On the 21st Sept 1846, before J.P. of King William Co., appeared SARAH ELLIOTT a resident of sd county, aged 85 years, and made declaration that she is the widow of WILLIAM ELLIOTT who was a corporal in CAPT. THOMAS BAYLOR's Co. of artillery in the Revolutionary War, and that her husband the sd WILLIAM ELLIOTT served as she understood for 3 years in sd. war, and after being disch'g'd from regular service he was drafted and had to serve in the militia one or two tours; that she does not know at what period he entered or left the service - nor the no. of his regt. All she knows he told her before he died, which was in above mentioned co. of Capt Baylor and in regt. of Col. Harrison. She knows of no one living who can vouch for his service. She married sd WILLIAM ELLIOTT on 15th Feb. 1786 and WM ELLIOTT died 15th Dec. 1814. Their marriage took place in sd Co. of King Wm prior to 1st day of Jan 1794. That she is unable from infirmity to attend Court. That she engaged RO. B. GAINES to prosecute her claim and supposed until lately that he had presented it.

              her
     Signed   SARAH X ELLIOTT
             mark

Before me THOMAS ROBINSON J.P.

The above is endorsed and testified to by ROBERT POLLARD, Clark of

Rejected Pension Applications   (continued)

WILLIAM ELLIOTT

Court of King William Co., who affixed the seal of the county and signed the paper. 31st day of Dec. 1846

Discharge of WM. ELLIOTT is attached.
"WM ELLIOTT a corporal of Capt. Pierce's Co. of Artillery commanded by Col. Harrison having served his term of Enlistment is hereby discharged from the services of U.S. his behavior as a good soldier merits the respects and esteem of all trew friends (sic) of their country.
Given under my hand the 20th of december at Camp in Morristown

         ED. CARRINGTON, Di Cor
         Con. I.R. Aty

This is to certify that WILLIAM ELLIOTT serv'd in the sd regt the term of three years.

         THOS. BAYTOP,
         Capt. Art'y.

A copy.   Auditor's Office Nov 13th 1783

         CHA. JONES. Clk.

         Executive Dept. Richmond, Va.
         May 13, 1847

The foregoing is a true copy of a paper filed in this department.
         Teste
         WM. H. RICHARDSON, Secy Com'th

Discharge and all other of above on one sheet of paper together.

Another sheet. Affidavit of a daughter of SARAH and WILLIAM ELLIOTT, made on 1st July 1847, in City of Richmond, repeats much that is in the first application paper, but in addition mentions that her mother, SARAH ELLIOTT died the 23 January 1847; and that she had heard CAPT YANCY LIPSCOMB say that her father was corporal in the Revolution. She believes Capt. Lipscomb was in the same regiment as her father. She, the daughter, was about 15 or 20 years old when her father died, which she says was in 1803. She also mentions "old MR JAMES WHITLOCK" who knew her father's service and that he died sometime before SARAH WILLIAMS

      signed   ANN BOSHER

Certified by JAS. C. WINGFIELD, J.P. of Henrico Co., and signed by CHAS. HOWARD, C.C. Henrico Co.

Rejected Pension Applications   (continued)

WILLIAM ELLIOTT.

Another paper is an affidavit made by MARY G. HILLIARD of the County of King William, the 3rd day of June 1847, before THOMAS ROBINSON, J.P. of sd Co., swears she is one of the children of WILLIAM and SALLY ELLIOTT, deceased, of aforesaid Co. That her father died when she was a child and that she only knew what her mother had told her.

                          Signed   MARY L. HILLIARD   (sic)

Another paper drawn up by RO. POLLARD, Clerk of Court, states that WILLIAM ELLIOTT died forty odd years ago, and that he knew MRS. SALLY ELLIOTT very well before her death and believes everything she stated about her husband's service to be true. Pollard states that he, himself, is now 64 years old and quite well acquainted with everyone in his community, and is quite sure there is only one Revolutionary soldier left in the County who can vouch for Elliott's service, and that is old MR DAVID VALENTINE.
    "Given under my hand and seal in King Wm. Co. this 3d day of June, 1847.

                                  RO. POLLARD   C.C.

Copy of Marriage Bond of WILLIAM ELLIOTT is attached:
"Know all men by these presents that we WILLIAM ELLIOTT and ANN LIPSCOMB are held and firmly bound unto the Commonwealth of Virginia in the just and full sum of 50 lbs Current money, to which payment well and truly to be made, which we bind ourselves our heirs, Exors and adms. firmly by these presents Sealed with our seals and dated 31st day of Jan 1786.
    The condition of the above obligation is such whereas the above WM ELLIOTT hath this day obtained a license for his marriage to SARAH LIPSCOMB daughter of JAMES LIPSCOMB, dec'd. Now if there is no lawful cause to obstruct the sd. marriage then the above obligation to be void or else to remain in full force and virtue.

                            WILLIAM ELLIOTT   (seal)
                            FRANCIS GRAVES   (seal)

Test
      JOHN QUARLES

State of Va. King Wm. Co. to wit: I ROBERT POLLARD, Cl of Ct of King Wm. Co. in Va. do certify that the above is a true transcript in the files of my office . . . etc. Dated 13 Mch 1847.

Another paper drawn by RO. POLLARD Clk says that he certifies that BENJ. R. BLAKE is an acting magistrate for that county (King Wm) 16 day of December 1847.

Another paper attached is affidavit of JAMES WHITLOCK's widow. She

Rejected Pension Applications (continued)

WILLIAM ELLIOTT.

states that JAMES WHITLOCK was a Revolutionary Pensioner of that County and died during the past year. Dated 4 Dec. 1847.

signed FRANCIS X WHITLOCK
(her mark)

Made before BENJAMIN R. BLAKE, J.P.

BENJ: TRUSLOW (this name may be THURLOW?) makes deposition that he knew WILLIAM ELLIOTT as a corporal for 3 years, etc., being a Rev. soldier himself and a pensioner. States he is 85 years old. Sworn before WM. FITZHUGH, J.P. Evidently made in Stafford County since JOHN M. CONWAY was C.C.

POLLY MADISON of King William County testifies that she was born and raised in WILLIAM ELLIOTT's neighborhood and knew of her own knowledge that he served in the war. Testimony given at the home of ROBERT BURKE in sd County, 1st Sept 1847 before FENDALL GREGORY, J.P. of sd County. States that she, POLLY MADISON, is 81 years old. She did not know his officers' names, but says a man by name of DANIEL LIPSCOMB, who was an officer who was killed in the service by <u>Our own men</u>, went out about the same time as Elliott. She also recalls that JOHN HOUTCHINGS enlisted and went out about the same time.

The name of Elliott's Captain was Baytop instead of Baylor as there was no such officer in the regiment of Col. Harrison, etc., etc. The old lady's memory is excused.

Signed R'D BURGESS,
agent for claimants,
Washington City.
31 October 1848.

ROBERT BURKE testifies to the character of POLLY MADISON, and in turn FENDALL GREGORY, the justice, testifies to Burke's character.

Further affidavits concerning character of POLLY MADISON are given by her neighbors in King William Co., on 16th Nov. 1847.

signed by
JOHN PEMBERTON
REUBEN A. HILLIARD
EDMOND LITTLEPAGE
WILSON C. PEMBERTON

And they in turn are given high recommendation by RO. POLLARD C.C.

THOMAS ROANE certifies that he has known MISS POLLY MADISON and lives in her neighborhood. Dated 22d Nov. 1847.

Rejected Pension Applications   (continued)

WILLIAM ELLIOTT.

J. CLEMENTS of Georgetown, D.C. acted as agent for MRS. SARAH ELLIOTT at one time.

A letter headed "Fleetwood", King and Queen County, Virginia, 17th May 1847, written by R. SAUNDERS to the Secretary of War, goes over SARAH ELLIOTT's claim again and states she did not know ROBERT B. GAINES had not attended to her claim until a communication adressed to the home of MR. R.T.M. HUNTER revealed the fact. Etc.

The testimony of a WM. C. ELLIOTT is referred to but is missing in the envelope of papers. They do not state his relationship, but religiously say Mrs. Hilliard and Mrs. Bosher are daughters.

End of ELLIOTT's Papers.

* * * * * *

JAMES KELLY

Rejected Pension Application
No. R. 5841

State of Virginia. Caroline County. 23 Sept. 1840. MRS. ELIZABETH KELLY personally appeared, she being a resident of the county and aged 74 years, and declared she is the widow of JAMES KELLY, deceased, a soldier of the Revolution who served in the Continental line about 3 years. That he was in the seige of Yorktown and present at the surrender. She swears she was married to JAMES KELLY the 24th of June 1786, and that her husband, the aforesaid JAMES KELLY, died the 24th of June 1811, and that she has remained a widow ever since. Sworn before WILLIAM R.B. WYATT, J.P.
Teste JOHN S. PENDLETON, Cl. Ct.

Another paper says ELIZABETH KELLY now of the County of Hanover and that her husband was of Caroline Co. Deponent states he is 54 years old and was well acquainted with JAMES KELLY of Caroline Co. and that Kelly was a drummer boy in the Revolutionary War in the regular service. He does not know when JAMES and ELIZABETH KELLY were married

Rejected Pension Applications (continued)

JAMES KELLY

but states they had children older than deponent. Dated 6 Sept. 1847.

signed WILLIAM X SOUTHWORTH
(his mark)

Before ELDRED CHEEN (?) J.P. Caroline Co.

JOHN SOUTHWORTH of Caroline County also makes deposition Oct. 1847, before ROBT. B. CORBIN, J.P. States he was born in Caroline Co. and knew JAMES KELLEY well and also his wife who was ELIZABETH CRUTCHFIELD. That they were legally married before 1st January 1794, because deponent lived but a short distance from Elizabeth's father. That she now lives in Hanover Co. That Kelley was believed to be a Drum Maj. in the Revolution. That Elizabeth's father Crutchfield was on 1st Jan. 1794 living on the land of old MR. WILLIAM SUTTON. Deponent was not more than 12 years old at that time and that his own father was also in the Revolution.

State of Virginia. County of King William

Deposition of SALLY D. LEWIS, who was SALLY D. SUTTON before marriage, now 70 years old, taken 14 June 1847 at her husband's, CAPT. ROBERT LEWIS, in King William Co. Says she is well acquainted with ELIZABETH KELLEY who was ELIZABETH CRUTCHFIELD. That she now lives in Hanover County and is the widow of JAMES KELLEY late of Caroline Co. She also says that James' father lived on deponent's father's land for 14 years and that her father often stated that Kelly had been a drummer boy in the Revolution and served 6 or 7 years. She says he was a good musician and that she has often heard him beat his drum and play his fife.

Deposition made before CHRISTOPHER TOMPKINS, J.P. of King William Co.
ROBERT POLLARD, C.C.

End of KELLY's papers.

* * * * * *

Rejected Pension Applications   (continued)

JAMES SHEPPARD

Rejected Pension Application
No. W. 7631

PRISCILLA HAY widow of JAMES SHEPPARD. Certificate of Pension issued 6 June 1854 and sent to W.A. SAUNDERS, Shackelford, King and Queen Co., Virginia, under Acts of Mar. 3, 1843 and June 17, 1844.
(above is on jacket)

Letter from RO. B. GAINES to SECY. OF WAR JAMES T. EDWARDS encloses record of marriage of JAMES SHEPPARD and his wife PRISCILLA - who after his death married GIDEAN HAY and is now the widow of said GIDEAN HAY. He asks return of said "register".

Another small folder says:
PRISCILLA HAY, dec'd., formerly widow of JAMES SHEPPARD, King and Queen Co., Va. Admd July 7, 1838 etc. 2 yrs. Segt of Artillery @ 120 per annum from Mch 4, 1836 to Mch 18, 1844, when she died. Pay to WILLIAM SAUNDERS adm for benefit of CATHERINE DAVIS (1), FRANCES RICE (2), THOMAS HAY (3), JOHN HAY (4), RICHARD B. HAY (5), JAMES C. HAY (6), ROBERT HAY (7), and SARAH ANN HAY (8), surviving children.
    Send cert. to WM. A. SAUNDERS, Esq., Shackelford, King and Queen County, Virginia.

Another small folder labeled "Brief of case of PRISCILLA HAY, widow of JAMES SHEPPARD, King and Queen Co. Record of service sustained by affidavit of DAVID BUTLER, and record of marriage by CHRISTOPHER JOHNSON, MAY DAVIS, etc for identity". THORNTON TRIPLETT is given as "Examining Clerk", which may mean that he, Triplett, was in Washington at the Pension Dept.

R. SAUNDERS writes a letter from Shackelford, King and Queen Co. 8th Aug. 1854, to HON. L.P. WALDO, Com. of Pensions, saying he is requested by the Admr of the estate of MRS. PRISCILLA HAY, etc (said admr being WM. A. SAUNDERS) to write the letter concerning her pension.

Another letter from Shackelford and written by R. SAUNDERS, states that JAMES SHEPPARD was sergt in artillery company of Capt. Spillers, and referring to "enclosed affidavit" of DAVID BUTLER a very old and respected man", who states that he knew Sheppard intimately from his childhood and although young at the time, he remembers perfectly that

Shepard enlisted and was in Capt. Spiller's Co. of artillery. He also encloses certificate showing that Sheppard rec'd on 26 May 1783 ₤. 84. 0. 10, which amount was paid to Capt. Spiller "As to reference to Capt. Spiller's rolls, it will be seen that he was from King Wm. Co." Letter also refers to evidence of RICHARD EUBANK who is a "highly respected old man whose veracity can be vouched for by persons of high standing in King Wm Co."

Another folder headed:
In King Wm. County Court, May 22, 1854.
It is ordered to be certified upon evidence of DAVID BUTLER and CHRISTOPHER TOMPKINS, (highly respected residents of this County) that PRISCILLA HAY widow of GIDEON HAY and former widow of JAMES SHEPPARD, and at her residence in this County (died) on the 18th of March 1844, leaving the following surviving children, towit: CATHERINE DAVIS, wife of PLEASANT DAVIS, FRANCES RICE, widow of RICHARD S. RICE, THOMAS HAY, JOHN HAY, RICHARD B. HAY, JAMES C. HAY, ROBERT HAY, and SARAH ANN HAY. That CATHERINE DAVIS and FRANCES RICE were the only two children by the 1st husband and the remaining six were children of second husband GIDEON HAY.

On the motion of WILLIAM A. SAUNDERS who made oath and together with WILLIAM S. BROOKE, WILLIAM D. TURNER, and BRECKIN (or BUCHIN) RICHARDS his securities entered into and acknowledged a bond in the penalty of $2000., conditioned as the law directs, which bond is ordered to be recorded, certificate is granted to said WILLIAM A. SAUNDERS for obtaining letters of administration on the estate of PRISCILLA HAY, dec'd.,
I JAMES OTWAY POLLARD, Clerk of the County Court of King William Co., do certify that the foregoing are true copies, etc.

                    Signed
                         J.O. POLLARD, C.C.
                         May 25, 1854

Another affidavit repeats much of former papers but in addition states that DAVID BUTLER is now 85 years old (7 April 1854) and was born and raised in King William County and has continued to reside there to the present time. Says he well remembers that JAMES SHEPPARD had a brother EDWARD at the place called Butlers old fields in King William County and in sight of deponents present residence, and that he remembers seeing them marching before they entered actual service. That JAMES SHEPPARD married PRISCILLA GENTRY soon after the war and sometime after removed to the adjoining county of Hanover where he resided for several years, and then returned to the County of King William where he continued to live until he died. And that after his death his widow married GIDEON HAY who has since died, leaving Priscilla and several children. And subsequently she also has died. That JAMES SHEPPARD was born and raised in King William County not a

Rejected Pension Applications (continued)

JAMES SHEPPARD. (continued)

great distance from deponent's home

              his
             DAVID X BUTLER
              mark

CHRISTOPHER TOMPKINS, J.P. certifies to honor and vericity of Butler. States that he (Tompkins) is now, 1854, 68 years old and has known Butler all his life.

Certifiacte is attached from Richmond, State Auditor's office, from a list of soldiers of the Va. State Line, who settled their accounts and rec'd certificates for the balance of their pay, and settlement was made 26 May 1783 in the name of JAMES SHEPPARD as sergeant of artillery for ₤ 84. 0. 10

Marriage bond of JAMES SHEPPARD dated 15 April 1785. JOHN SATTERWHITE signs with James. "The condition of the above obligation is such that whereas the above JAMES SHEPPARD hath this day obtained a license to marry PRISCILLA GENTRY, daughter of JOHN GENTRY", etc. etc.
Teste J. QUARLES

          Signed JAMES SHEPHERD (seal)
                JNO. SATTERWHITE (seal)

Bond is certified by J.O. POLLARD, J.P. of King William Co.

A very interesting yellow and frayed booklet marked "Memorandum Book for JAMES SHEPPARD for the year of our Lord 1792". Contents almost illegible. Appears to be accounts. The name WM WODEY appears frequently in such manner (and many others copied below).

  WM WODAY to one half Bush Cone   Jan. 5, 1792
  WM WODEY to one Barel Cone   Jany 17
  MATT PAGE one half Barel Cone   Jany 18
     one hundred Bundles foder Do
     one half barel cone Do
  WM WODAY to one half barel Cone   Jany 22
      etc.

Other names appearing:
  WM ROCK (or KOCK)
  NATHAY PAGE
  MATHEW PAGE (all these may be abbreviations of MATTHEW
   PAGE)
  JOSHEWAY DAVIS
  GEORGE CLARKE
  JOHN SATEWHITE
  MANN PAGE
  AMBROSE LIPSCOMB
  MATHEW PAGE

Rejected Pension Applications (continued)

JAMES SHEPPARD (continued)
Other names appearing (continued)

    ALISHUA TALEY
    GEORGE CULP
    JAMES PARKER
    THOMAS FOSTER
    JAMES OLIVER
    EDWARD CLARKE
    JOHN PASLEY
    JOHN PARSLEY
    EDMOND CLARKE
    WM MANSON
    ROBERT JOHNSON
    WM COCK
    JAMES LIONS
    ROBERT FLEMING

For year 1793
    EDWARD CLARKE
    JAMES LIONS
    JAMES OLIVER
    WM TALEY
    CHARLES HUNDLEY

For year 1794
    GEORGE THOMAS
    WM HOOPER
    WM NONE
    NELSON HUDLEY
    DOCTOR LIONS
    JAMES OLIVER
    PATRICK FOULER
    WM HOOPER

    "JAMES SHEPHERD to four quarter beafe - 60"
    WM HAYES to side beafe - 123
    EDWIN FLEET 1 quarter beaf - 70
    GEORGE THOMAS 20 May 1804
    GEDEON HAY, May the 20 1804.

RICHARD RICK and FANEY SHEPHERD was married August 7, 1816

RICHARD BURRUSS born Mch 20 1815. Son of GEORGE and FRANCES
    BURRUSS

        Notes from JAMES SHEPHERD's Account Book

            (continued next page)

Rejected Pension Applications   (continued)

JAMES SHEPARD   (continued)
Notes from JAMES SHEPARD's Account Book.   (continued)

```
To account of wood 1794
     WILLIAM CHRISTON              5 loads
                                   2
                                   4
     DOCTOR MARCHANT              31 Do
```

JAMES NELSON, Hanovertown

JOHN HAY the son of GIDEON MESILA HAY was born July 27, 1797
THOMAS HAY   was born Oct. 20, 1799
RICHARD HAY   was born Feb. 8, 1801
JAMES HAY   was born Sept. 8, 1803
ROBERT HAY   was born Jan. 10, 1805
SALEY HAY   was born Sept. 2, 1808
These are the ages of my children

GIDEON HAY evidently took possession of the book or else
Priscilla did.

```
WM SHEPARD to JAMES SHEPARD fifteen shilings lent    15
8 shilings pade PETER FOSTER                          8
46 to SAM BIRDE 3 for wine                           46
```
                    (page cut off here)

BENJERAM TOLER, By Credit for one and sixpence   1. 6

JAMES SHEPHERD was mared in the yeare seventeen hundred and 86
MARY SHEPHERD was born Febuary 8, 1787
FRANCES SHEPHERD Was Borne Febuary 17, 1789
NANCY SHEPHERD Was Borne Nov 5, 1791
NANCY SHEPHERD died Sept. 31, 1793

                    (End of Account Book)

Another folder among papers headed "New Shackleford, King and
Queen 26 May 1853, mentions that RO. B. GAINES is now deceased.

    A certification of RICHARD EUBANK states that he was born
in the County of King and Queen, a short distance from the
village of Ayletts, and that he is 89 years old (it being 25
Oct. 1853).
Certificate made in King William County.

Rejected Pension Applications (continued)

JAMES SHEPARD (continued)

A "Declaration" by WILSON CARY NELSON, J.P. and made by PRISCILLA HAY. Repeats much of foregoing but adds that she was married to JAMES SHEPHERD in April 1786 and that he died in 1800. That she will be 75 years old on 22 of August 1839. Date of declaration is 19 June 1839.

End of SHEPHERD Papers

* * * * * * *

ROBERT BRUMFIELD

King William County, Virginia
Rejected Application No. R. 1365

On 28th Jan. 1835 appeared personally before RICHARD WILSON, a Justice of the Peace of King William County, ROBERT BRUMFIELD aged 80 years on 24th of June last and stated that he enlisted in the State Service of the U.S. Revolutionary Army for 3 years, under CAPT. HARRY QUARLES of King William County, at Maj. Burwell's Mill, and marched from thence to Little York through New Kent County; was stationed there sometime, then marched to a place called Hillsborough in he believes South Carolina - and later was marched on further and was present at Gates' defeat. Sometime later was returned to Little York where he remained until his discharge, having served his 3 years. The date of his discharge he cannot remember as he is so old and mentally and bodily weak. He enlisted in fall of 1776 or 1777. After being at home from his first discharge for sometime he was drafted into Militia service of U.S. under CAPT. RICHARD DABNEY of King William County, and met at King William Courthouse on or about 5th day of January 1781 and marched from there to Holt's Forge; from thence to Bacon's ordinary, and from thence to Williamsburg, and from thence to Portsmouth, back to Williamsburg and there discharged after having served a tour of two months. He was again ordered out by draft under CAPT JOHN QUARLES and met at Hanover Courthouse about 5th day of May 1781 and from there marched to Four Mile Creek below Richmond City, and from thence to Malvern Hills on James River and from thence to Charles City County, where he remained until discharged, having served this time a tour of 2 months. He was again ordered by draft under Capt. Abrahams and met at Frazer's Ferry in King William County on or about 20th Oct. 1781, and marched from thence to a church in Gloucester Co. and from thence to Ludel's ordinary, then to Gloucester Point, and then to West Point where he was discharged having served 2 months,

35

Rejected Pension Applications   (continued)

ROBERT BRUMFIELD   (continued)

making in all a service of 3 years in the State Service and 6 months in the Militia.

He was in skirmish at Ludel's ordinary and one at Gloucester Point and was at the siege of Little York. He remembers the following officers ("field officers") under whom he served at different times: MAJ. ARMSTEAD, COL. HOLT RICHESON, COL. TAYLOR, COL. ENNIS, COL. DABNEY, but he cannot remember the regiment he was in. He was paid by the regiment pay-master for his time in the State Service, but never was paid for the 6 months in Militia. He has been afflicted for last 12 years and did not know until about 12 or 15 months ago that he was entitled to a pension as a soldier of the Revolution.

He was born in Cumberland County, Virginia, from which county he was removed at about age of 6 years to county of King William. where he has lived ever since. His brother WILLIAM BRUMFIELD was in State Service with him in same regiment but had enlisted a short time before he did. He has no record of his age. He took the Oath of Allegiance. THOS. W.S. GREGORY, WILLIAM NEWMAN, THOS. PEMBERTON and ALEXANDER KING, residents of King William County are living in his neighborhood and know said Brumfield and can testify to his character, veracity and that he served in the Revolution.

                                         his
                        Signed   ROBERT X BRUMFIELD
                                         mark

Sworn and subscribed to before me
RICH'D WILLEROY   J.P.

We, THOS. W.S. GREGORY and ROBERT MYRICK, residents of King William County, are well acquainted with ROBT. BRUNFIELD, etc., etc. (vouching for his veracity - age - and reputation as soldier of the Revolution.

Brumfield, in answer to questions, replies that he was born in 1754.

At bottom of above document the County Clerk, ROBERT POLLARD certifies that RICHARD WILLEROY, ISAAC COCK, JAMES FOX and JOHN SKYRON, Esquires, are magistrates of King William Co.
Dated 11 February 1835.

2nd paper attached.
HEZEKIAH SPENCER, resident of King William Co., aged 76 years, Testifies that he knows Brumfield and that he is very poor and ill, and entitled to a pension. Dated 28th May 1834.
This testimony was given before ROBERT HILL, J.P. of King William Co.

A letter, dated 19 Feb. 1835, to JAMES L. EDWARDS of the Pension Office and signed WM. P. TAYLOR. Does not state who he is and no residence given. Appears to be a lawyer perhaps handling the matter for the soldier.

Rejected Pension Applications   (continued)

ROBERT BRUMFIELD   (continued)

JOHN TALIAFERRO, resident of King William Co., says he is 71 years old, and testifies that he knows ROBT. BRUMFIELD served in the Revolutionary War for he was with him for one of his 2 month tours in the Militia. Dated 29 Jan. 1835. Made before ISAAC COCKE, J.P. who vouches for Taliaferro's reputation as a creditable citizen.

A letter headed King William Courthouse, 17th March 1835, to JAMES L. EDWARDS, Commissioner of Pensions states that "Through the HON. WILLIAM P. TAYLOR, a member of the last Congress", etc., and goes on to say there is'nt the slightest doubt that ROBT. BRUMFIELD served in the War, as all his old friends in the county insist he did. Says the poor old man is nothing more than a child now, can neither eat, drink nor walk without assistance, having had a stroke of palsy some years since. The letter asks that certificate be sent to ROBT. BRUMFIELD at Endfield P.O., King William Co. This letter signed by RO. B. GAINES.

A second paper by HEZEKIAH SPENCER states more positively that he knew ROBT BRUMFIELD during the Revolution and knows positively that he enlisted and served at least 2 years and perhaps 3 in the U.S. Army and that after he returned home from this service Spencer saw him in the Militia service. Dated 10th Feb. 1835. Made before RICHARD WILLEROY, J.P.

RACHEL JARVIS of King William County, aged 75 years the 10th day of November 1834, testifies that she was born and raised in King William County, in the neighborhood where ROBERT BRUMFIELD lived, and was well acquainted with him during the Revolutionary War, and knows he served at least 6 months in the Militia Service. Dated 2nd February 1835.
Made before JAMES FOX, J.P.

Affidavit of DAVID VALENTINE of King William County, Virginia, aged 73 years on the 15th April next (1835).
Says he knew ROBERT BRUMFIELD during the Revolution and knows he served as a Militiaman on a tour of 2 months because he (Valentine) was with him in the Militia service.
Made before JOHN SKYRIN, J.P.

A second declaration by ROBERT BRUMFIELD says Maj. Burwell's Mill where his 1st Company assembled was in King William Co. That he thinks Hillsborough is in North Carolina. He now thinks he enlisted in 1776. He now says the church in Gloucester County where they

Rejected Pension Applications. (continued)

ROBERT BRUMFIELD   (continued)

camped was Ware Church, and they went from there to Sewel's ordinary. This second declaration is largely repitition of the first and was made before JOHN SKYRIN, J.P. Dated 28 May 1834. THOMAS W.S. GREGORY, this time with WILLIAM H. DUGAN, both say they are residents of King William County and know Brumfield.

Another declaration by Brumfield was made 27th of March 1834 before ROGER GREGORY, J.P. of King William Co. It is largely repitition of the other declarations but says they went to Ware River in Gloucester Co., and to Sewell's Tavern. This time he refers to THOMAS MOSS, JAMES SMITH and STERLING LIPSCOMB as his neighbors who can vouch for him.

Aug. 27th 1834.   RACHEL JARVIS made another affidavit before JAMES FOX, J.P.

EDMUND BEADLES of King William County, aged 70 years on 31st day of August 1834 testifies that he knew Brumfield well during the Revolution, living at that time in the same neighborhood. Dated 27 August 1834.
Made before JAMES FOX, J.P.

A second letter from RO. B. GAINES, "King Wm C.H., Va.". dated 31st March 1835, expresses dissatisfaction with the way the department is handling Brumfield's case.

A letter to R.B. GAINES, Esq., from the Pension Office points out discrepancies in Brumfield's claims, viz. that his name is not found on the rolls of CAPT. HARRY QUARLES company. Signature illegible.

Evidently Vice President Martin Van Buren asked for a report on Brumfield's case. A copy of a letter to him is filed with the papers. It gives the same reason as above - that Brumfield's name is not on CAPT. HENRY QUARLES' rolls. Dated 17 Feb. 1835.

HON. J.J. ROANE wrote 16 June 1835.

                End of BRUMFIELD papers

LOYALIST CLAIMS

THE MEMORIAL OF MR. RICHARD CORBIN, JUN'R.
Late of Virginia

Manuscript Division, New York Public Library, New York City.
American Loyalists.
Audit Office Transcripts. Volume 59. page 226

The Memorial of Mr Richard Corbin Jun'r
late of Virginia

Sheweth
    That your Memorialist in 1783 presented a Memorial to you x x (then follows a long statement concerning amended values) x x.
    Your Memorialist is the son of MR RICHARD CORBIN who was for many years one of his Majestys Council and Deputy Receiver General of his Majestys Quit Rent Revenue in Virginia. In the year 1772 Your Memorialists father put him in compleat possession of an Estate called Moss's Neck and Rich Land in the County of Caroline x x x when in the year 1775 the preval'ce of the Faction put an end to all his prospects. In Nov'r 1774 your memorialist with the utmost difficulty escaped the personal resentment of the popular Faction to whom his known attachment to the British Government had made him obnoxious. In 1775 open Acts of Rebellion manifested themselves in the province and the Rebels compelled the Receiver General to pay as much of his Majesty's Money as would replace a quantity of Gun powder that had been removed from the Magazine by the Governor. The constant attachment of your memorialist to the British Cause And his open and determined Opposition to its Enemies Obliged him at this time to quit his Country and his Friends. And to him was committed the charge of bringing to England such Bills as could be saved From the popular fury. These were deposited to a large amount with MR. OSGOOD HEMBURY who transacted all the business for the Deputy Receiver.
    x x x x by the Citizen Laws passed during the War in America and since the Revolution he is considered as an Alien and incapable of holding property by Descent or purchase or of having it held in Trust for him x x x his return to his Native Country is for ever prohibited and nothing can more fully manifest that he can expect no Assistance from thence than this Circumstance that for four years he has languished in the Walls of a prison without receiving any support except that which has obtained from the Bounty of the British Government x x x x . Your Memorialist begs to make one remark on the Cause of his Confinement above alluded to, that the Support and Assistance necessarily given to two Brothers and three Nephews in this Country and his hopes during the time he was affording the Assistance that the Events of the War would have a different aspect x x x x x.

Loyalist Claims   (continued)

MR. RICHARD CORBIN, JR. late of Virginia (continued)

Volume 59. page 235
Papers also include:

February 12th 1787

Evidence on the foregoing Memorial of RICHARD CORBIN
The Claimant sworn
Memorial read
He Confirms the Truth thereof on Oath
Certifiacte to his Loyalty from Lord Dunmore read

    Is a Native of Virginia. In 1774 he resided with his Father in Williamsburgh who was Receiver General and a Member of his Majesty's Council. The Claimant acted as his private Secretary. His Father remained there during the War being a very old Man. He never took part with the Americans, but was obliged to conform. The Claimant as early as 1774 declared his Sentiments in favour of Great Britain and thereby rendered himself so obnoxious that he was under the necessity of quitting the Country in August 1775. He brought home Lord Dunmore's dispatches.
    Says he was very much persecuted before he left Virginia and was near being tarred and feathered.
    Being asked if his Father approved of his avowing his sentiments in favour of Great Britain, says he did. The whole Family were loyal.
    He arrived in England in September 1775 and has been here ever since.
    He received an Allowance of ₤ 150. per Annum from the Treasury from 1775 to 1783, since which time he has received only ₤ 100.
    Says Lord Dartmouth informed him after Lord Dunmore came away, that it was his Majesty's Intention to appoint his Father Governor in case the people returned to their Allegiance.
    Says he has not heard from his Father since the Conclusion of the peace.
    He is not the eldest Son. His elder Brother JOHN TAYLOE CORBIN is in the Country.
    Says it was on September 14th 1772 that he was put in possession of the property mentioned in his schedule.
    The land lay in St Marys Parish Caroline County. From the time he was put in possession he had the entire Mannagement of the Estate and received all the profits thereof to his own use. He received them up to 1775. The net profit of the Estate was from 12 to ₤ 1500 Cur't per Annum. Very near half the Land was in Cultivation and it lay upon the Rappahannock a Navigable River. Its produce was Tobacco, Indian Corn and Wheat. There was a pretty good House on it with necessary offices, (and) there were two dist'o dwelling Houses. He is of the opinion the 1959 Acres of Land would have sold for ₤ 10. Currency per Acre selling the whole Estate together in 1775.
    The Meadow Land adjoined. Thinks that would have sold for ₤ 20.

Loyalist Claims (continued)

Mr. Richard Corbin, Jr., late of Virginia. (continued)

Currency per Acre
Thinks upon an Average the Negroes would have sold for ₺ 50. Curr't each. x x x .
All this property x x devised to him by Will and he would have come into Legal Possession of it on his Fathers Death.
The last time he heard of his Father was by Letter dated the 29th July 1786, he was then alive x x x
x x x
Refers to the affidavit of WILLIAM GRAHAM produced Viz't:
WILLIAM GRAHAM formerly an Inhabitant of Virginia being sworn on the Holy Evangelists of Almighty God, deposeth and saith that he hath known RICH'D CORBIN Esq'r son of the HON'BL RICHARD CORBIN formerly one of his Majestys Council for the Colony (now the State) of Virginia for many years past and particularly at the time of the said RICH'D CORBIN the Youngers leaving Virginia in the year 177t x x x that the said RICHARD CORGIN the Younger always was a x x x a loyal subject x x x and held in utter detestation those measures of his Countrymen which finally terminated in the Subversion of the British Government in America.
This Deponent further saith that having lived for many years in the Family of the said RICH'D CORBIN the elder this Deponent hath at different times made sundry Wills for him and in all of them x x two of the Estates of the said RICHARD CORBIN the elder called Moss's Neck and Rich Land Plantations lying in Caroline County on the River Rappa between the Towns of Port Roy'l and Fredericksburg were invariably devised to his son RICHARD x x x .
This Deponent further saith that the two elder Brothers of the said RICHARD CORBIN the younger who were married and had Children were in possession of some Estates and receiving the profits of the Father's permission and a well grounded Expectancy that such Estates would be confirmed to them upon his Death by his last Will and Testament, it being the general Intention of the said RICHARD CORBIN the Elder, x x not to divest himself of the absolute Rights of property in his Estates during his own Life time x x x .
(WILLIAM GRAHAM further states that to avoid squestration of Moss's Neck and Richland, RICHARD CORBIN, Sr., instructed him to draw a new will the exact wording of which he could not remember)

Signed   WM GRAHAM

Sworn before the Commissioners of American Claims at their Office Lincoln Inn Fields June 16th 1786

RICHARD LEE   Clerk

page 243. Certificate (on oath) of GEORGE TURNER. Says those Estates (Moss's Neck and Richlands) have been under his care and management

Loyalist Claims (continued)

Mr. Richard Corbin, Jr., late of Virginia   (continued)

for 14 years last past, etc., "was considered as the property of RICH'D CORBIN Jun'r Esqr., he visited it 3 or 4 times a year gave Orders as Master and received and paid all untiil the year 1775)
Dated 4 August 1786. Signed GEO. TURNER

page 245. "Mr Corbin says he x Believes his Father now holds the Estates in his own Hands and that he has devised it entirely away from him (the Claimant) Delivers in the following Extracts from Letters he has received from America respecting his Inability to take an Estate in Virginia

Virginia Sep'r 5th 1786
I send you an Attested Schedule of that particular part of your Patrimony which you have lost by your fatal Desertion from your Native Country and your no less imprudent unfortunate attachment to the King of Great Britain.
By the Citizen Laws of this Country passed pending the War and since the Revolution you are considered an Alien and consequently incapable of holding Land either by Descent or purchase. By your improvident by your insane Attachment to that unjustifiable System of Coercion which the half Tyrant Minister of England adopted against the Liberties of your Native Country you have rendered yourself so extremely odious to all ranks of people as to make a temporary return only for the purpose of seeing your aged Father with one foot in the Grave before he dies a step not only inexpediant but even dangerous to yourself and injurious to those of your Family who by their consummate prudence and caution have been hitherto able to stem the Torrent of popular Odium it would be infandum renovare Dolorem Could the Right of Citizenship be obtained for you it would be fortunate but this is a Thing wild even to think of, the door being once opened among the many that might rush in who knows but that Arch Traitor Arnold might be one - passions and prejudices run as high as ever and your Restoration to your Country or property is Impracticable"

page 247. The sworn statement of MAJOR JOHN RANDOLPH GRYMES includes:
"knew the Claimant in Virginia and that he was obliged to quit the Country on account of his Loyalty. They were going to tar and feather him which was the immediate Cause of his coming away".
"In 1774 he resided at his Fathers and was then considered as the Master of a very fine Estate called Moss's Neck and Richland. It was notorious in the Country that it was Col. Corbins Custom to put his Children in possession of the Estates he designed for them, reserving the Right in himself in order (as he supposes) to ensure Obedience". x x x.

Loyalist Claims   (continued)

WILLIAM GRAHAM

Manuscript Division,
New York Public Library, New York City.
American Loyalists. Audit Office Transcripts.
Volume 59.   page 78.

The Supplemental Memorial
of William Graham

Humbly sheweth
That your memorialist did by his Claim preferred on the 19th day of February 1784 refer to certain Papers which he had requested to be sent to him from Virginia x x x .

Remarks

For some years after I obtained a Licence to practice the Law in Virginia, I attended only the Court of Middlesex County, but about the years 1771 or 1772 I began to extend my Practice and gave Attendance at the Courts of Gloucester and King and Queen Counties as well as Middlesex.
In August of the year 1772 upon the Death of the Gentleman under whose Instruction I had at first Applied to the study of the Law, I succeeded to a considerable Part of the Practice which had been in his Hands, and from that Period considered myself as established in Business"
(then follows an estimate of loss in fees, etc.)

page 85.

March 29th 1786

Evidence on the foregoing Memorial of WILLIAM GRAHAM
The Claimant sworn
  Swears to the truth of his Memorial
  He is a Native of Scotland. Went to America in 1763.
  Produces a Certificate sign'd RICH'D CORBIN dated 24
      Sep'r 1784 to his having been disarmed and having
      refused to take the Oaths
  Says Mr Corbin was one of the Kings Council and is now
      a Resident in America.
  Certificate of LORD DUNMORE to his belief of his Loyalty
      x x x .
  "Produces a Copy of a Resolve of a Committee of the County
      of King and Queen directing that the Claimant with
      others should be disarmed for refusing to take the
      Oath to the state. Dated 14th June 1776
  Says he was advertised in the papers as "a Person inimical
      to the liberty of America".
  That he was discharged from the Court in Gloucester
      County. Could

Loyalist Claims (continued)

WILLIAM GRAHAM (continued)

> not leave the country for lack of money, was enrolled in the Militia and was obliged to pay a substitute to serve for him, etc.

THE MEMORIAL OF MRS. ARIANA RANDOLPH

Manuscript Division.
New York Public Library, New York City.
American Loyalists, Audit Office Transcripts.
Volume 58. page 614.

The Memorial of MRS ARIANA RANDOLPH Relict of JOHN RANDOLPH Esqr late His Majestys Attorney Gen'l of Virginia.

The evidence in this claim submitted by MAJOR JOHN RANDOLPH GRYMES includes:

"Produces an Official Extract from the Commons of the Will of EDMUND JENNINGS deceased (Father of Mrs Randolph) date 10th March 1756 whereby he devises to COLONEL RICHARD CORBIN of Virginia ₤ 1000 Sterling in trust to place the same out at Interest and pay the Interest to his Daughter ARIANA RANDOLPH for her use during her Life, and after her Death to pay the same to his Grandson EDMUND RANDOLPH if he should survive his Mother but if not he directs the same to be equally divided among his Granchildren surviving her x x "

Loyalist Claims (continued)

THE MEMORIAL OF THE REV. SAMUEL HENLEY
1787

Manuscript Division.
New York Public Library, New York City.
American Loyalists.
Audit Office Transcripts.
Volume 59, page 425.

> The Memorial of Samuel Henley
> Clerk, late Professor of Moral
> Philosophy in William & Mary
> College   Virginia

Papers in the claim include:

> "March 27th 1787

Evidence on the foregoing Memorial of the Rev'd SAML HENLEY
The Claimant Sworn
Memorial read. He confirms the Contents thereof

> A Native of England. Went to Virginia in 1770 - was
> professor of Moral Philosophy in William and Mary College
> when the Troubles broke out, was then in orders.
> When the Troubles began he did every thing in his Power
> in support of the British Government and was thereby laid
> under the Necessity of quitting his Situation having
> rendered himself obnoxious to the Americans.
> He quitted Virginia the 24th May 1775 and came to England.
> His salary as Professor was ₤ 125. Sterling per Ann:
> The Perquisites ₤ 50. Sterling per Annum
> Says his Books were Packed up and left by him under the
> Care of MR JOHN WATSON who intended to have sent them by
> one of the last Ships but they were stopped by the Committee of York Town and after being kept a long time in
> their Warehouse were returned to the College where they
> were consumed by fire for the most Part.
> The few which were saved he has Received Payment for from
> MR JEFFERSON at a price fixed by himself which is about
> ₤ 30."

THOMAS WEBB TO MRS. MARY WEBB
1783

Note: This letter does not appear to be an American Revolutionary item. However it is. See Virginia Colonial Abstracts, Volume 5. pages 1 to 10. The original has been, mistakenly, included in the collection of papers of my great uncle John Rutherfoord, formerly Governor of Virginia, and now (1942) in the Manuscript Division in the Library of Duke University, Durham, North Carolina. These papers are so perfectly taken care of by Dr. Tilley at Duke that it is a relief and satisfaction to find them there. The Rutherfoord papers were turned over to Duke University by my beloved and delightful Cousin Nannie Johnson (Mrs. Bradley Saunders Johnson), a grand daughter of Governor Rutherfoord, who was indeed overburdened with the care of innumerable historic papers, portraits, miniatures, silver, furniture, etc., etc. The Rutherfoords had no connection with the Webbs so far as I know. The few Webb papers in the collection evidently had been disposed of by Judge Francis Wyatt Smith, of "Smithfield", King and Queen County, about the same time that the Rutherfoord papers came to Duke University and were placed with them.

            Beverley Fleet.

The following memo. will explain my own connection with these papers and how I happen to know of them.

```
CAPT. WM. FLEET'  | PRISCILLA FLEET
   "Goshen"       |     m
   K.& Q. Co.     | JAMES SMITH of
                  |   "Smithfield"
                  | He was nephew and
                  | heir of JAMES WEBB
                  |   (Webb Papers)
                  |
                  | JAMES ROBERT FLEET    | J.R. FLEET   BEV. FLEET
                  |    "Goshen"           |      m
                  |                       | ANNA RUTHERFOORD
                  |
                  | 11 OTHER CHILDREN.
                  |
THOS. RUTHERFOORD'| JOHN RUTHERFOORD, Gov. of Va. etc.
  of Richmond.    |      (Rutherfoord papers)
                  |
                  | WM. RUTHERFOORD       | ANNA RUTHERFOORD
                  |                       |      m
                  |                       | J.R. FLEET
                  |                       |        BEV. FLEET
                  |
                  | 11 other children.
```

Rather a rigamarole. But I want to explain how and why I know of these originals. The letter follows on the next page.
                     B.F.

Thomas Webb to Mrs. Mary Webb   (continued)

London Sept'r 1783

My dear Sister
    Since my arrival from Curacoa in this Country my Health has grown worse. I went on my first arrival to the Hot Wells of Bristol in order to drink the Waters and breathe the Air of that Place but a great deal of bad weather that we had whilst I was there prevented my receiving any Benefit and I returned here a few Days ago in a low State as I have ever been.
    I shall embark in about two Days for Lisbon which my Friends recommend in Preference to the South of France and from the favorable Accounts I have received of the purity of that air I have Hopes to recover my Health, should I fail I shall hardly expect to see you again. From thence you may expect to hear from me.
    Pray keep the Boys constantly to their Studies, as it is the only means of making clever Fellows of them which I ardently wish.
    Tell Jemmy I received his Letter dated in June which I will answer from Lisborn.
    Writing now gives me Pain.
    In Sickness or Health I shall allways remain

Your most affec't Brother
THO'S WEBB

Addressed:

   MRS MARY WEBB
   Essex County
   near Hobbs Hole
   Virginia.

Note: Had he only known that the Red Sulphur Springs, the White Sulphur Springs or the Hot, in his own native Virginia were the places for him instead of wet England and far away Lisbon - but no doubt, they were at that day, too crude for a wealthy and ill gentleman. Of course no letter came from Lisbon, this was the end.   B.F.

PETITION OF THE PAMUNKEY INDIANS
1786

Archives Division.
Virginia State Library, Richmond, Va.
King William County Petitions
7 December 1786.

To the honourable the Speaker and House of Delegates.
The Petition of the Indians on Pamunkey River, humbly sheweth
That your Petitioners under an Act of Assembly have always had Trustees appointed by your honourable House to protect them in their Persons and Rights.
The Gentlemen last appointed being all dead except MR CARTER BRAXTON who is now removed out of the County
Your Petitioners are left destitute of any Friends to apply to in cases of Need.
They therefore humbly pray that the following Gentlemen may be added to Mr Braxton who we wish may remain as one of our future Trustees, DRURY RAGSDALE, JAMES HILL, THOMAS LITTLEPAGE and JAMES JOHNSON jun'r. and your Petitioners as in duty bound will ever pray

Endorsed: Pamunkey Indians
             their peto
             dec'r 7th 1786
             ref'd to props
             reasonable
                rep
                bill

Note: My great great grandfather, William Munford, came to Richmond in 1803, and having married a daughter of Col. William Radford, built the house, now destroyed, at the N.W. corner of 5th and Canal Streets. My mother remembered the house well. It sat high from the street, was entered by way of long steps the yard held by a retaining wall. A room in the English basement, with a seperate entrance, had been set aside for the use of a decayed gentlewoman, for such was the term of the day. This old lady had 18 cats. They customarily sat in dignity around her in a ring, except:
Once a year everything was removed from the large parlor. The Queen of the Pamunkey Indians arrived, wearing that absurd crown presented by Charles II to her tribe, now to be seen at the John Marshall House in Richmond. She came, accompanied by her braves, to pay the yearly tribute to the Governor of Virginia. The tribute was Virginia game. A deer, so many brace of wild duck, wild turkeys and so on. This party took possession of the parlor. Deer skins were spread upon the floor. At night the queen lay down in the center and the braves lay around her, feet out and their heads touching some

Pamunkey Indians (continued)

part of her body. At the slightest sound, the barking of a
dog, anything, they were on their feet facing out, the queen
in the center.
    To the distress of my great great grandmother, never did
the Queen arrive, but that old lady's 18 cats, ordinarily so
self contained and so dignified, must select that moment for
a general and violent cat fight in the back yard, set all the
dogs in the neighborhood howling, gread great grandpapa, night
shirt, night cap and slippers out curseing, kicking and throwing
his Latin Grammer at them, while the hostess attempted to explain
to the Queen and her alert braves that it was nothing at all
but Mr. Munford's peculiar way of spending the night.   B.F.

Note No. 2
Then again, this past year I'm being driven by an aristocratic
Richmond chauffer (very black) down through that part of the
country. A school was breaking up down there in the bushes.
I agreeably remarked ' I never saw so many nice looking colored
children'. The driver speaking in confidence, one gentleman to
another way off in the country, replied 'They aint no niggers
attall. They aint nothin but Indians!'
So -   B.F.

Further note: Now that colored people can have straight hair
at a price from any drug store, why bother with the dirty,
slovenly, drunken Indians, or boast of Indian blood? Why
indeed?   B.F.

Final Note: It is a far reach from the ring of braves, with
bows bent and arrows drawn around their queen, while old Mr.
Munford threw his book at the cat fight to 1942. Even within
the last 125 years the Pamunkey Indians have become as nothing.
From the early settlements of the English, a friendly tribe,
mere peace and protection wrought swifter ruin than hundreds
of years of bloody warfare.
    Recently some God-fearing woman, interested in the revival
of ancient Virginia folk lore, arranged a celebration in Richmond of the Pamunkies. True to announcement in the papers, a
handful of them (quite negroid) appeared - all dressed in Sears-
Roebuck Indian costumes, danced dances plainly taught them by
modern school mistresses and exhibited arts and crafts, also
supervised by modern school mistresses, that would have been
a disgrace to a primary school
    In 1942 there is practically nothing left of the Pamunkey
Indians. The tribe has been almost absorbed by the local
negroes (the chauffeur nevertheless to the contrary), the
fragment remaining completely disintegrated.   B.F.

ITEMS FROM VIRGINIA TREASURY RECEIPTS

Archives Division,
Virginia State Library, Richmond, Va.

Cash Book, 1770-1776
Treasurers Office, Virginia.
Pages not numbered.

Account headed:

DR. EDM'D PENDLETON Esq'r Speaker of the Convention

```
1776 April 26    To Cash for 1/4 yrs allowance      100. -. -
     June   9    To Cash for 1/4 yrs allowance      100. -. -
     Octr   9    To Cash for 1/4 yrs allowance      100. -. -
     Decr  18    To do as president of the Convention
                    to 6th of Oct                    40. -. -
           19    To do 1/4 years allowance          100. -. -
```

Account headed:
HON'BLE EDM'D PENDLETON Judge of the High Court Chancery

1778 Sept 17 To Cash   125. -. -

Account headed:

Cash rec'd of Sundry Gentlemen for the use of the
Delegates deputed to the General Congress

```
1774 Augt        To Cash rec'd of COLO GEO BROOKE (K&Queen)
                                                    15. -. -
1775 June 19     To MR LYNE (King and Queen)        15. -. -
     July  1     To COLO DIXON for Williamsburg     15. -. -
```

* * * * * *

Cash Book. 1777-1778
Treasurer's Office. Commonwealth of Virginia.
page 31.

Account headed: The Treasury Cash Account. Entries include:

```
1777 May    9    To Publick Salt Acco'tt of COLO  )
                 GEORGE BROOK for K & Queen. 250  )  163.10.10
                 To the Ex'rs of WILL'M FLEET for )
                 PHILL ROOTS Sherriff K & Q 1765  )
                 by COLO GEORGE BROOK             )   64. 9. 4
                 To The Adm'r of JOHN ROBINSON    )
                 Esq'r by COLO GEORGE BROOKE      )  613. 6. 10
```

50

Virginia Treasuary Receipts   (continued)

Cash Book 1777 - 1778.
page 49.

1777 June 28   To Tax on Writts and Marriage   )
                Licences since Aug't 1775 to 1 April)
                1777 of THOS G. PEACH Clerk of   )
                Amelia by B M.   )   23. 2. 0

page 52
1777 June 28   To the Adm'rs of JOHN ROBINSON)
                dec'd of COLO GEO: BROOK   )   2275. -. -

page 59.
1777 Agu'st 6   To Admors of JNO ROBINSON rec'd)
                on Loan of GEO BROOKE Esq   )   864. -. -
1777 Ag'st 6   To WILLIAM TODD rec'd on Loan of)
                GEORGE BROOKE Esq   )   132. -. -

page 63.
1777 Sept 2   To the Army rec'd of WHITAKER CAMBELL)
                for balance of recruiting Acc'o   ) 114.12. -
1777 Sept 2   To Loan Office rec'd of CORBIN GRIFFIN 290. -. -

page 65.
1777 Sept 10   To Wheel Carriages rec'd of JNO HILL)
                Shff of King William   )   74. 2. -

page 80.
1777 Nov 5   To Tob'o Insp'n rec'd of Quarles and)
                Mantapike Insp'n per GEO BROOKE   )   2.11. 8
     Nov 5   To Loan Office rec'd of JNO   )
                ROBINSONs Admrs per GEORGE   )
                BROOKE   )   300. -. -

page 81.
1777 Nov. 6   To Insp'n of Tob'o rec'd of Temple)
                and Scott Insp'n at Todds and   )
                Ayletts per JAMES TURNER   )   4.15. -

page 84.
1777 Nov 20   To Army rec'd of AMBROSE DUDLEY balance)
                of recruiting Money returned   ) 13.18. 6

page 94.
1778 Jany 3   To Loan Office rec'd of Admors of)
                JOHN ROBINSON   )   1000. -. -

Virginia Treasuary Receipts   (continued)

Cash Book 1777 - 1778

page 98.
1778 Jan'y 17   To Marriage Licenses rec'd of)
                 R'D TUNSTALL Clerk of King &)
                 Queen   )   11.15.1 1/2

page 107.
1778 Mar 2d   To Debts squestered rec'd of JAMES)
                 CAMPBELL & Co.   )   324.16. 8

Treasuary Department Cash Book.   1777 - 1779.
Book marked inside: "GEORGE WEBB Treasurer
                            15th January 1777
                            Account of Cash received
                            into the Treasuary".

page 57.
1778 Mar 7   To Quit Rents rec'd of JOHN ORELL)
                 TUNSTALL by the hands of JAMES Mc)
                 CRAW for the County of Halifax for)
                 1773 and 1774   )   382. 9. -

page 61.
1778 Mar 24   To Acco Cards rec'd of COL. GEORGE)
                 BROOKE for 36 pc Cotton at 15/ and)
                 17 pc Wool at 12/ sold in King and)
                 Queen   )   37. 4. -

page 61.
1778 March 25   To Arrears of Shffs rec'd of COL   )
                 WILLIAM LYNE Shff for taxes collect-)
                 ed in King and Queen County for the)
                 years 1773 and 1775   )   86.18. -

page 65.
1778 April 7   To the Army rec of COLO VIVION   )
                 BROOKING by the hands of JOHN TABB)
                 Esqr as a Ballance overpaid him   )
                 for the County to the Drafts of   )
                 the County of Amelia   )   20.12. 6

52

Virginia Treasuary Receipts   (continued)

Cash Book 1777 - 1779.

page 121.
1778 Oct 26   To tax on marriage and ordinary Licenses)
               granted in King and Queen from last day)
               of Oct 1777 to 1st In'st rec'd of RICH'D)
               TUNSTALL Clk per Acct audited   )   25.13. -

page 133.
1778 Decem 5   To Quit Rents received of COL GEO BROOKE)
               by the hands of BERNARD TODD for balance)
               of Quit Rents collected in King and)
               Queen County for the year 1769   )   78.12. -

               To Ditty received of JOHN WARE by the)
               hands of BERNARD TODD for balance of)
               Quit Rents collected in King and   )
               Queen County for the year 1770   )   108.19. 7

               To General Assess'm rec'd of THOMAS)
               COLEMAN high Sheriff of King and   )
               Queen by the hands of McCANDLISH   )
               and TODD in part of Taxes collected)
               in that County for this year   ) 2818.17. -

page 135.
1778 Dec 9   To Quit Rents rec'd of WILLIAM LYNE)
               Esq late Sheriff of King and Queen)
               for balance of Quit Rents collected)
               in the years 1772 and 1773 and the)
               full amount of Quit Rents for the   )
               year 1774 per Commiss. Return from)
               Kg and Qu.   )   227.19 2 1/4

page 148.
1779 Feb 3   To Sequestered Debts rec'd of HONBLE)
               B. WALLER Esq by the hands of JOHN T.)
               CORBIN, Esq. on acco. of JOHN JACOB)
               of London Druggist Cer No 4   )   111.10. 8

page 165.
1779 March 16 To RICHARD CORBIN Esq. rec'd of him)
               by the hand of ROBERT PRENTIS Esq.)
               being balance of the Revenue of 2/)
               per hhd per Auditors Cert   ) 4111.14. 5

PETITION OF WILSON LUMPKIN

Archives Division,
Virginia State Library, Richmond, Va.
King and Queen Co. Petitions, 20 Dec. 1827.

To the Hon'ble the General Assembly of the Commonwealth of Virginia

The petition of WILSON LUMPKIN of King and Queen County respectfully represents that he served Three years as a soldier in the revolutionary army in the company of CAPT GREGORY SMITH of the 7th Virginia Regiment and that he has not rec'd compensation for this service more than his common daily pay.

That his bounty of Land was sacrificed after trying every reasonable and available means to have it secured.

That by industry and frugality, and hard labor, he had acquired a comfortable fortune, which he enjoyed for many years. That at the time revolutionary soldiers were placed on the pension list by an act of Congress, for that case made and provided, he felt himself precluded from takeing the oath prescribed by law, by reason of the prosperity of his situation and thus could not throw himself upon the bounty of his country

But your petitioner in his old age, has experienced a most unexpected and fatal reverse of fortune in yielding to those tender and parental ties, which bound him to his offspring, parental solicitude for the well fare and prosperity of his only son induced your petitioner, to aid him by the loan of money, and the credit of his name to establish him as a merchant. That your petitioners son after living many years as Clerk to Messrs Haxhall & Co (sic) left the City of Richmond for the Town of New Orleans in the state of Louisana where he met an untimely grave, and your petitioner has not been able to obtain any satisfactory information of the property left by his son at his death or to receive any part of the sum loaned but on the contrary is reduced to poverty and want.

Your Petitioner is now aged infirm and indigent and throwing himself upon the magnamity and liberality of your honorable body, he prays that you will grant him some compensation for past services in the revolutionary war, by placing him on the pention (sic) list upon the same footing as other soldiers, and your petitioner will ever pray etc.

WILSON LUMPKIN

(Body of petition and signature in same handwriting which is that of an educated man)

Endorsed:
WILSON LUMPKIN's/ petition/ EDWIN UPSHAW/ Dec'r. 20th 1827/ ref'd to Claims/ 1828 Jany 5th/ Laid on table/ 11th Rejected/ 14 Reported/ King and Queen.

THE GLEBE - CEMETARY INSCRIPTIONS

The Glebe, The house now, 1942, standing and in good condition and ownership, for Drysdale Parish, is near Newtown in the upper part of King and Queen County. There are four stones in the small cemetary just back of the dwelling house. Somewhat overgrown with vines and shrubs they also are in good condition.
B.F.

RICHARDSON LUMPKIN
1797
Juno 26, 1868
A poor sinner saved by the blood
of Jesus Christ

In Memory
of
MRS P.T. LUMPKIN
wife of
RICHARDSON LUMPKIN
Born Jany 13th 1813
Died March 23rd 1842

In Memory of
MARIA JOSEPHINE
wife of
E.J. GRESHAM
Born April 16th 1832
She lived a consistent christian
and died peacefully
on November 16th 1856
Aged 24 years and 7 months

In Memory
of
ANN CATHERINE
wife of
B.F. GRESHAM
Born Nov'r 29th 1829
Died calmly and peacefully
the death of the Righteous
Nov'r 8th 1857
Aged 27 years 11 months and 9 days

ROANE TO HENRY
1786

Archives Division.
Virginia State Library, Richmond, Va.
Executive Papers, 1786.

Letter addressed:

>His Excellency
>PATRICK HENRY Esqr

>Richmond, Octo. 3, 1786.

Sir,
    I hereby beg Leave to resign the seat which I have the Honor to hold, in the privy council.
    As it is my highest gratification to serve my country to the utmost of my power, so nothing could induce me to relinquish at this Time, this important Trust, but an indispensable obligation on me to recur to the profession for which I was educated.
    I am with the highest Respect for your Excellency and the honourable council.

>Y'r mo. obed't. serv't.
>SPENCER ROANE

His Excellency the Governour

Endorsed:
>Mr Roanes letter
>of resignation

Note: We wonder what the redoutable Pat thought of that? You don't suppose he told his devoted son-in-law, who he saw through so clearly, to write it, do you?   B.F.

MILITIA
1793 - 1799

Archives Division,
Virginia State Library,
Richmond, Virginia.

Fourth Division composed of four Brigades viz.

    2nd Brigade composed of 6 Regiments
    8th Brigade composed of 6 Regiments
    9th Brigade composed of 7 Regiments
   14th Brigade composed of 8 Regiments

14th Brigade was composed of 8 Regiments. These were made up from the following counties: Essex, King and Queen, Gloucester, Northumberland, Richmond, Mathews, King William, Lancaster, Middlesex and Westmorland.
Of these the regiment designated as the 9th was from King and Queen.

HENRY LEE, Major General of the 4th Division.
HENRY YOUNG, Brigadier General of the 14th Brigade.
BEVERLEY ROBINSON, Brigade Inspector 14th Brigade.

On a Roll dated 26 August 1794 the following appear as of the 9th Regiment and from King and Queen County.

The Roll is headed "Numerical Rank Roll of the Field officers of the Militia of Virginia, formed and returned in obedience of the General Orders of the 15th of August 1794"

Rank Name
 45   PHILIP PENDLETON (under list of Lieu. Cols. - Commandants)
                         Marked "Resigned"

Lists on pages following carry dates to Sept. 1800.

Includes:

140   JOHN HOSKINS (As well as I can judge from the lists he
                       was a major) List marked: "Commission
                       dated Jany 2nd 1799"

128   THOMAS C. MARTIN, Major, dated 26 Aug. 1794.
                               Marked "Resigned"

The following marked as Majors and dated 2 Sept 1794

248   ROBERT HOSKINS   Transferred to N R
343   WILLIAM FLEET   refused to act
359   JOHN KIDD   deceased
417   THOMAS BAGBY
423   THOMAS BAGBY

Militia, 1793 - 1799 (continued)

A Register of the officers of the fourth Regiment of Cavalry in the fourth Division of the Militia January 1st 1797

Names	Rank	County	Date of Commission
LARKIN SMITH	Lieut Col Comm'dr	K & Q	Feb 17 1796
WILLIAM TEMPLE	Captain	K & Q	Dec 20 1796
JOHN TEMPLE	2nd Lieutenant	K & Q	Dec 20 1796 Removed

* * * * * *

Organization of the Militia 1797.
page 43.

King and Queen
9th Regiment
January 1st 1797

Names	Rank	Date of Commission	
PHILIP PENDLETON	Lieut Col Comm'dr	May 6, 1793	Resigned
JOHN HOSKINS	Major	March 12, 1794	promoted
ROBERT HOSKINS	Major	June 20, 1796	
JOHN KIDD	Captain	March 12, 1794	promoted
LYNE SHAKLEFORD	Captain	do	removed
THOMAS BAGBY	Captain	do	Promoted
SAMUEL HOSKINS	Captain	do	Dec'd
WILLIAM HOSKINS	Captain	do	Deceased
RHODERICK STERLING	Captain	do	Resigned
TEMPLE GWATHMEY	Captain	do	Resigned
BAYLOR FLEET	Captain	do	
JOHN WEDDERBURN	ditto Lt Inf'y	May 21, 1796	Removed
HUMPHREY WALKER	ditto	do	
CUTHBERT TUNSTALL	ditto Lt Infy	June 20, 1796	Resigned

Militia, 1793 - 1799 (continued)

King and Queen, 9th Regiment, January 1st 1797 (continued)

Names	Rank	Date of Commission	
PHILEMON BIRD	Capt. Lt. Infy	June 20, 1796	
DAWSON COOKE	Lieutenant	March 12, 1794	promoted
WILLIAM SHAKLEFORD	do	do	do
WILLIAM GRESHAM	do	do	do
HUMPHREY TEMPLE	do	do	Resigned
THOMAS COLLINS	do	do	
ROBERT BOYD	Lieu. Lt. Infy	May 21, 1796	promoted
JOHN TEMPLE	do	do	Refuses to Act
JOHN BAGBY	do	June 20, 1796	promoted
JAMES JONES	do	do	Removed
JOHN RICHARDS	do	do	
WILLIAM GRESHAM	do	do	
THOMAS DEW	do	do	promoted
WILLIAM DIDLAKE	Ensign	March 12, 1794	promoted
RICHARD T. SHAKLEFORD	do	do	do
ROBERT JEFFRIES	do	do	do
JOHN HILL	do	do	do
JOHN BOYD	do	do	
WILLIAM MORGAN	do	May 21, 1796	promoted
ROBERT B. HILL	do	do	do
BENJAMIN GAINES	do	June 20, 1796	do
WILLIAM BOYD	do	do	do

Militia, 1793 - 1799 (continued)

King and Queen, 9th Regiment, January 1st 1797 (continued)

Names	Rank	Date of Commission	
KAUFFMAN WATTS	Ensign	June 20, 1796	Refuses to accept
PHILIP PERRYMAN	do	do	
EDWARD WRIGHT	do	do	promoted
BEVERLEY ROBINSON	do	Augt 9, 1797	Resigned
ROBERT BOYD	do	do	promoted
ROB'T B. HILL	do	do	
WILLIAM MORGAN	Lieut Lt Infy	do	
RICHARD CORBIN	Ensign Lt Infy	do	promoted
WILLIAM BOYD	Lieutenant	do	promoted
JOHN HILL	do	do	removed
JOHN SEGAR	do	do	
THOMAS JEFFRIES	Ensign	do	Promoted
JOSIAH RYLAND	do	do	
BENONI CARLTON	do	do	Promoted
JOHN HOSKINS	Lieut Colo Com'r	January 2, 99	
WILLIAM FLEET	Major	do	refused to accept
THOMAS ROANE junr	Captain	do	
JOHN BAGBY	Capt L Infantry	do	
BENJAMIN GAINES	Lieut L Infantry	do	
HENRY GARNETT	Ensign do	do	refused to accept
JOHN KIDD	Major	June 3, 1799	deceased
WM SHACKELFORD	Captain	do	

60

Militia, 1793 - 1799 (continued)

King and Queen, 9th Regiment, January 1st 1797 (continued)

Names	Rank	Date of Commission	
DAWSON COOKE	Captain	June 3, 1799	
THOMAS DEW	do	do	
RICHARD T. SHACKLEFORD	Lieutenant	do	
WILLIAM DIDLAKE	do	do	Resigned
EDWARD WRIGHT	do	do	
BENONI CARLTON	do	do	
ZACHARIAH SHACLLEFORD	Ensign	do	
JOHN BLAND junr	do	do	
HENRY GARNETT	do	do	Promoted
ROBERT GARRETT	do	do	
LARKIN DESHAZO	do	do	
ROBERT BOYD	Capt Light Inf't	do	
RICHARD CORBIN	Lieut do	do	
RICHARD HILL	Ensign do	do	

Note: Of course it is evident that entries were made on these lists after the original date, in fact additional entries on other lists along with these shown here are dated as far forward as Sept. 1800.   B.F.

CAPT. RICHARD CORBIN's
ARTILLERY COMPANY, 1812

Archives Division,
Virginia State Library,
Richmond, Va.
Virginia Muster and Pay Rolls, 1812.
Vol. 1. pp 45 - 46

Endorsed: Cap't Rich'd Corbin
                          of
                   King and Queen
                       County
                        1813
                    Muster Roll

Large sheet headed:
"Muster Roll of a Company of Artillery of the line of Virginia Militia Commanded by CAPT RICHARD CORBIN call'd into actual service under the Gen'll orders of the 6th February from the Commencement of Service to the 3rd day of May 1813 inclusive"

Throughout the Muster Roll all are shown as "Commencement of service Arrival at Rendezvous" as of 13 February 1813. Also all are shown as "Distance from home to Rendezvous" 15 miles, which is, on the face of it impossible. There is a colume "Names present" which duplicates the names on the roll. Looks to me like a forerunner of much modern accounting - duplication of effort and ink wasted.   B.F.

No.	Names	Rank
1	RICHARD CORBIN	Captain
2	THOMAS C. HOOMES	First Lieutenant
3	JAMES GRESHAM	Second Lieutenant
1	THOMAS W. TODD	First Sergeant
2	ARCH'D R. HARWOOD	Second Sergeant
3	FRANCIS ROW	Third Sergeant
4	THOMAS F. SPENCER	Fourth Sergeant
1	PHILIP B. PENDLETON	First Corporal
2	CHARLES S. HENRY	Second Corporal
3	JAMES MITCHELL	Third Corporal
4	GEORGE B. FLEET	Fourth Corporal
1	THOMAS G. CRITTENDEN	Private
2	DANIEL WATTS	"
3	THOMAS MILBY	"

Capt. Richard Corbin's Artillery Company, 1812   (continued)

No.	Names	Rank	No.	Names	Rank
4	JOHN FLEMING	Private	37	THOMAS FLEMING	Private
5	RICHARD PEMBERTON	"	38	SPENCER ROANE	"
6	JAMES C. NEW	"	39	HENRY CLARKE	"
7	CAMPBELL BURTON	"	40	JOSIAH THOMAS	"
8	WILLIAM WYATT	"	41	THOMAS WILLIAMS	"
9	WILL T. SHACKELFORD	"	42	ALEX: P. MUSE	"
10	RICHARD MOORE	"	43	ALEX FRAZER	"
11	ELIJAH BRUSHWOOD	"	44	THOMAS BULLMAN	"
12	CHRISTOPHER EUBANK	"	45	CLEMENT PYNES	"
13	JOHN EUBANK	"	46	WILLIAM MORRISS	"
14	RICHARD WALDEN	"			
15	JOHN ROANE	"			
16	STERLING CORR	"			
17	WILLIAM JACKSON	"			
18	JAMES CORR	"			
19	AMBROSE JACKSON	"			
20	WILLIAM EUBANK	"			
21	ROBERT TRICE	"			
22	WILLIAM WALDEN	"			
23	CHARLES COLLIER	"			
24	AMBROSE DURHAM	"			
25	GEORGE C. JEFFRIES	"			
26	JOHN BARTLETT	"			
27	ELIAS BURTON	"			
28	THOMAS WATTS	"			
29	JOHN ORRILL	"			
30	THOMAS PEMBERTON	"			
31	JAMES BRUSHWOOD	"			
32	ROGER PALMER	"			
33	THOMAS M. JEFFRIES	"			
34	JAMES GAINES	"			
35	JACOB D. WACKER	"			
36	THOMAS DOUGLAS	"			

Capt. Richard Corbin's Artillery Company, 1812   (continued)

No.	Names	Rank
47	RICHARD WYATT	Private
48	RICHARD GAINES	"
49	DUDLEY DIGGS	"
50	JOHN HEMINGWAY	"
51	WILL RICHASON	"
52	CHRISTOPHER SHACKLEFORD	"
53	GEORGE C. NEW	"
54	ELLIS CARLTON	"
55	JOHN F. DRABELLE	"
56	FRANCIS F. STUBBS	"
57	DAV: JUDAH	"
58	JOHN W. DUNN	"
59	WARNER EUBANK	"

* * * * *

CAPT. THOMAS FAULKNER's
COMPANY
1812
(1814)

Archives Division,
Virginia State Library,
Richmond, Virginia.

Virginia Muster and Pay Rolls, 1812
Vol. 3, Page 44

Endorsed: Receipt Roll of
             Cap't Tho's Faulkners Co.
                  $ 2398.54
                  Duplicate

Pay roll receipted. JAMES H. ROY, paymaster of 61st Reg't.
March 25 to June 28. 1814 limiting dates. The name JOHN B.
ROBERTS appears as witness to most of the men's signatures.
Also the names GOULDMAN SMITHER, ANDREW L. MOORE, GEO HOSKINS,
THO NEWCOMB, JAMES JONES, WILLIAM WATKINS, PHILIP WATKINS SEN.,
and WM WHITLOCK as witnesses.
   Mans names and amounts receipted for shown below. Precise
dates

Capt. Thos. Faulkner's Company, 1812 (continued)

of service and other detail omitted. This may be obtained from the original.

No.	Name	Rank	Amount
1	THOS FAULKNER	Captain	128.
2	JOHN ALEXANDER	Lieutenant	95.
3	THOS. G. SMITH	Ensign	39.66
4	GEO. HOSKINS	Ensign	39.66
5	WM A. WRIGHT	1st Sergeant	35.20
6	THOS. DUDLEY	2nd do	35.20
7	LEOND WATHAN	3rd do	35.20
8	JOHN ROBERTS	4th do	34.83
9	ARCHIE BROWN	1st Corporal	32.
10	RO. SMITH	2nd do	32.
11	SAM MEREDITH	3rd do	32.
12	BROOKE HILL	4th do	31.66
13	ALLEN JOSEPH	Private	25.60
14	ANDREWS THOS. P.	"	25.60
15	ACREE WILLIAM	"	25.60
16	BIRCH VINCENT	"	25.60
17	BLAND RICHARD	"	25.60
18	BALL ARCHIBALD	"	25.33
19	CHAMBERLAYNE JOHN	"	25.33
20	COLLINS ZACHARIAH	"	25.60
21	COOKE HENRY	"	25.60
22	DILLARD WILLIAM	"	25.60
23	DILLARD JOHN	"	25.60
24	DUDLEY PAULIN	"	25.60
25	DUDLEY GEO. B.	"	25.60
26	DUDLEY RICHARD	"	25.60
27	DAME GEO. G.	"	25.60
28	DAVIS ANDERSON	"	25.60
29	DEDLOCKE JOHN	"	25.60
30	EUBANK THOS	"	10.13
31	FROMAN JOHN	"	25.33
32	FOGG THOMAS	"	25.60
33	FOGG NATHANIEL	"	25.60
34	FIGG WM. C.	"	25.33
35	FLEMING JNO	"	8.80
36	GREENSTREET JOSEPH	"	25.60
37	GAINES ROBT	"	25.33
38	GWATHMEY JOSEPH	"	25.33

Capt. Thos. Faulkner's Company, 1812 (continued)

No.	Name	Rank	Amount
39	HART CLAIBORNE	Private	25.60
40	HALL ROBERT	"	25.60
41	HAILE THOMAS	"	25.33
42	HEATH GEO.	"	25.33
43	LEEMAN JAS.	"	25.60
44	MINOR OWEN	"	25.60
45	MUIRE WM.	"	25.60
46	MILBY JOHN JR.	"	25.60
47	MEREDITH JOHN	"	25.60
48	MILBY WM. B.	"	25.60
49	MARTIN WILLIS	"	25.60
50	MILBY JAMES	"	25.60
51	MOORE ANDREW L.	"	25.33
52	NEWCOMB THOMAS	"	25.60
53	NUNN RICHD Q.	"	25.60
54	PRINCE ROBERT	"	25.60
55	PITTS BENJAMIN	"	25.60
56	PITTS TAYLOR	"	25.60
57	PATTERSON PHILIP	"	25.33
58	REYNOLDS POWELL	"	25.66
59	RICE RICHD S.	"	25.33
60	RICE SAML	"	25.33
61	ROWE ANDERSON	"	25.33
62	SLAUGHTER STEPHEN	"	25.33
63	SEARS PHILIP	"	25.60
64	SEARS THOMAS	"	25.60
65	SMITHER GOULDMAN	"	25.60
66	TUCK ROBERT	"	25.33
67	TUCK HENRY	"	25.33
68	TAYLOR EDMOND	"	25.60
69	THORNTON JAS. R.	"	25.33
70	TERRY CHAMPION	"	25.33
71	THOMAS JOHN	"	25.33
72	VAUGHAN JOHN	"	25.60
73	WATKINS PHILIP JR.	"	25.60
74	WATKINS PHILIP SEN.	"	25.60
75	WATKINS JOHN	"	25.60
76	WATKINS WM.	"	25.33
77	WALDEN JNO.	"	25.60
78	WHEELY THOS.	"	25.33
79	WIDGEON LEVIN	"	25.33
80	WALKER ROBT	"	25.60
81	WHITLOCK WM (son Jno)	"	25.33
82	WHITLOCK WM (son Jos)	"	25.33

Capt. Thos. Faulkner's Company, 1812 (continued)

No.	Names	Rank	Amount
83	WILLIAMS LEONARD	Private	25.33
	Captain's Servant	"	25.60
	Lieutenant's Servant	"	21.33
	Ensign's Servant	"	12.26
			- - - -
			2398.59

* * * * * * *

LEGAL PAPERS

HILL TO TOMPKINS AND HILL
1799

Fleet Papers.
BEVERLEY FLEET,
107 North Plum St.,
Richmond, Virginia.

THIS INDENTURE made this thirtieth day of March in the year of our Lord one thousand seven hundred and ninety nine Between WILLIAM HILL of the County of King and Queen in the State of Virginia of the one part and CHRISTOPHER TOMPKINS of the County of King William in the said State attorney in fact for JOHN W. SEMPLE of the State of Kentuckey. ISAAC ROBERTSON of the said State of Kentucky and EDWARD HILL of the County of King and Queen in the said State of Virginia of the other part WITNESSETH that the said WILLIAM HILL for and in consideration of the sum of one dollar of lawful money of Virginia to him in hand paid by the said CHRISTOPHER TOMPKINS ISAAC ROBERTSON and EDWARD HILL the receipt whereof he the said WILLIAM HILL doth hereby acknowledge, and for and in consideration of securing to the said CHRISTOPHER TOMPKINS the payment of a considerable sum or sums of money that is due and owing to the said JOHN W. SEMPLE from the said WILLIAM HILL, which became due in consequence of certain monies rec'd by the said WILLIAM HILL as executor etc of RACHEL ROBERTSON Dec'd and as guardian of LUCY SEMPLE wife of the said JOHN W. SEMPLE who was LUCY ROBERTSON child and devisee of the said RACHEL ROBERTSON dec'd also for and in consideration of securing to the said ISAAC ROBERTSON a certain sum or sums of money that is due and owing to the said ISAAC ROBERTSON which became due in consequence of certain monies rec'd by the said WILLIAM HILL as executor to the said RACHEL ROBERTSON dec'd and as guardian to the said ISAAC ROBERTSON, who was also child and devisee of the said RACHEL ROBERTSON dec'd and also for and in consideration of saving harmless the said EDWARD HILL and preventing him from paying any money or suffering as security to the said WILLIAM HILL in two bonds or specialties WILLIAM HILL and EDWARD HILL to EDWIN MOTLEY of the county of King and Queen aforesaid and in all other cases whatever where the said Edward is security for him he the said WILLIAM HILL hath granted, bargained and sold and by these presents doth grant bargain and sell unto the said CHRISTOPHER TOMPKINS, ISAAC ROBERTSON and EDWARD HILL and each of them severally and each of their heirs the following negroes to wit, Paris, Isaac, Bob, Dover, Zachara Jesse, James, Henry, Frank, Obediah, Ambrose, George, Ephraim, Edmond, Dandridge, Harwood, Vernon, London, Betty and her increase, Grace and her increase, Patience and her increase, Lucy and her increase, Cordelia and her increase, Mima and her increase,

LEGAL PAPERS

Hill to Tompkins and Hill   (continued)

Emma and her increase, Celia and her increase, Darcus and her increase, Hetty and her increase, Sally and her increase, Daniel and John, also one hundred and fifty barrels of indian corn, seven sorrel horses, four bay horses, one sorrel horse colt, one sorrel mare and her increase, one bay mare and her increase, one black mare and her increase, one black mare colt and her increase, thirty three head of cattle and their increase, thirty three head of sheep and their increase, twenty head of hogs and their increase, one riding carriage, two waggons and gear, one ox cart and gear, one tumbrel and gear, one wheat fan, one still, and the following houshold furniture, to wit, one desk, one book case, two mahogony tables, three walnut tables, fourteen walnut chairs, eight windsor chairs, ten feather beds, bedsteads and furniture, TO HAVE AND TO HOLD an absolute estate in the said negroes and their increase, the said horses and their increase, the said cattle and their increase, the said sheep and their increase, the said hogs and their increase, the said Corn, waggon, cart, tumbrel, still, wheat fan and household furniture, unto the said CHRISTOPHER TOMPKINS, ISAAC ROBERTSON and EDWARD HILL and to each of them and to their and each of their heirs Executors, administrators and assigns forever, provided always and upon condition, that if the said WILLIAM HILL, his heirs, Executors or administrators, do and shall well and truly pay to the said CHRISTOPHER TOMPKINS the aforesaid sum or sums of money that are due and owing from the said WILLIAM HILL to the said JOHN W. SEMPLE, also shall well and truly pay to the said ISAAC ROBERTSON the aforesaid sum or sums of money that are due and owing to him from the said WILLIAM HILL and also will save harmless the said EDWARD HILL and prevent him from paying any money or suffering as security for the said WILLIAM HILL in the two bonds aforesaid and in all other cases whatsoever where the said Edward is bound as security for the said William. - then in that case and from thence forth these presents and every thing herein contained shall cease, determine and be void, any thing herein contained to the contrary notwithstanding. And the said CHRISTOPHER TOMPKINS, ISAAC ROBERTSON and EDWARD HILL for themselves, their and each of their heirs Executors and administrators do covenant and agree to and with the said WILLIAM HILL and his heirs, and the true meaning hereof is, that until default shall be made in the proviso and condition herein contained he the said WILLIAM HILL and his heirs, shall and may remain in the possession of hold and enjoy the afore mentioned negroes, corn, stock, waggon, etc. and household furniture, and receive and take the profits thereof to his and their own proper use and benefit any thing herein contained to the contrary notwithstanding. IN WITNESS whereof the

LEGAL PAPERS

Hill to Tompkins and Hill (continued)

parties to these presents have hereunto set their hands and seals the day and year above written

Signed Sealed and delivered   WILL. HILL   (seal)
in presence of   CHRISTOPHER TOMPKINS (seal)
     EDWARD HILL   (seal)

BEVERLEY ROBINSON)   as to WILL HILL)
RO. HILL)   C. TOMPKINS)
JOHN HILL)   and E. HILL)

At a court held for King and Queen County at the Courthouse on Monday the 10th of June 1799 This deed of Mortgage indented was proved by the oaths of BEVERLEY ROBINSON, ROBERT HILL and JOHN HILL the witnesses thereto and is ordered to be recorded

     Teste

         ROBERT POLLARD C.C.

     A Copy
       Teste
         WILL TODD D.C.C.

Endorsed:

     HILL   )
      to   )
     TOMPKINS and)   Co. Mortgage
     HILL   )

       RO. HILL Ayletts

Note: Further papers concerning this group will be found on the following page under "Wainewright vs Hill".

LEGAL PAPERS

WAINEWRIGHT VS HILL ET AD

United States District Court,
Richmond, Virginia,
Ended Causes. File Box 26.

Abstract. Complaint of ROBERT WAINEWRIGHT and MARTIN PEARKES Exors of LATHAM ARNOLD dec'd a subject of the King of Great Britain.
That Arnold, being a merchant in London, had dealings of a large amount with JOHN HILL, WILLIAM HARRIS and WILLIAM HILL of the County of King William in Virginia, merchants and partners, carrying on a trade under the firm of Hill, Harris and Hill. That there was a balance due Arnold on 24 September 1776 of ₤ 1694. 7. 6 Sterling.
That the war intervened.
That JOHN HILL having died, suit was instituted against said WM HILL and WM. HARRIS and judt. obtained for $
(left blank in the original papers).
That WILLIAM HARRIS is in such circumstances that little or nothing can be recovered from him.
That WILLIAM HILL is possessed of lands, slaves and other property of considerable value, but so covered by prior incumberances that there is little prospect of receiving payment from him.
That JOHN HILL died "seized and possessed of a very considerable real and personal estate". That ROBERT HILL is exor of his will and the estate is liable for the debt. Requests the Court for relief, etc.
Bill of Complaint endorsed 1800.

Paper endorsed:

              ROBERT HILL Exor etc)
                        ad   )   Answer
              L. ARNOLDs Exors   )

The answer of ROBERT HILL, executor of the last will and testament of JOHN HILL deceased, a defendant to the bill of complaint exhibited against him and others, in the circuit court of the United States, in the District of Virginia, by ROBERT WAINWRIGHT and MARTIN PEARKES, executors of the last will and testament of LATHAM ARNOLD deceased, subjects of the King of Great Britain, complaineth
This defendant reserving to himself every benefit of exception to the imperfections of the said bill for answer thereto saith
That as to any debt for which this defendants intestate may have been liable to the said Arnold: he requires full and adequate proof: that he doth not admit the liability of his testator to the debt, stated in the said bill: that if however any claim can be sustained

LEGAL PAPERS

Wainewright vs Hill   (continued)

against this defendant, he requires that all the distributees
of the said JOHN HILL who died intestate, and to whom this
defendant hath allotted their respective shares of his estate,
be made parties defendants hereto, for the purpose of contri-
bution according to their just obligations: that these distributees are MARY HILL, the widow of the said JOHN HILL,
THOMAS WALKER who intermarried with, and has survived FRANCES,
a daughter of the said JOHN HILL: JOSEPH GWATHMEY and MARY
his wife: JOSEPH HILLYARD and ANNE his wife, another daughter;
TEMPLE ELLIOTT and AGNES, his wife, another daughter; ISAAC
DABNEY and SUSANNAH his wife, another daughter, and JOHN HILL
and BAYLOR HILL two other sons of the said JOHN HILL deceased:
that WILLIAM HARRIS, another defendant in the bill named, hath
lately departed this life intestate, and HENRY HARRIS his son,
hath taken out letters of administration on his estate: that
this defendant is advised, that the debts for which a mortgage
hereto annexed, was made on 30th day of March 1799 between
WILLIAM HILL a codefendant, and CHRISTOPHER TOMPKINS, ISAAC
ROBERTSON and EDWARD HILL, for a large amount of property,
hath been nearly if not fully discharged; and that for any
surplus beyond those debts, the said property is liable to the
execution of the complainants against the said WILLIAM HILL,
and ought therefore to be pursued, before any attempt is made
against this defendant.
   And this defendant denying all combination prays to be
hence dismissed with costs: without that that etc.

City of Richmond to wit
   Sworn to before me by the said ROBERT HILL, in due form
of law, this 8th day of November 1801

                              WM RICHARDSON Mayor

With these papers a summons: dated 22 Dec. 1800. Executed on
ROBERT HILL. Endorsed: "service   2.
                           30 miles   1.50
                                         - - -
                                         3.50

Also: Summons dated 16 July 1800, is endorsed:
              "R HILL   ELLIOTTS W. HOUSE"
       and   "Not found and a copy left in the Compting Room
              of ROBERT HILL with one of his clerks

                              BEN MOSBY DM
                                 for
                              D.M. RANDOLPH
                                   M D V

LEGAL PAPERS

Wainewright vs Hill (continued)

Summons. Dated 10 August 1803, to HENRY HARRIS, exor. of
WILLIAM HARRIS, deceased.
Endorsed: "Caira, Cumberland County. Not found"
Also another summond dated 16 December 1803. Same notations.

Memo: Suit dismissed by the complainants who acknowledge "to
have rec'd from RO HILL Exor of JOHN HILL a Bond for $5000.00
payable by Installment in satisfaction of his third part of
the D M in the Bill mentioned". No date.

* * * * * *

BEVERLEY TO NOEL

Letter Book of ROBERT BEVERLEY. 1794 - 1797.
Now, 1942, belonging to:
    BLAND BEVERLEY, Esq.,
    "Blandfield"
    Caret P.O.
    Essex County, Virginia

This letter from ROBERT BEVERLEY to CORNELIUS NOEL bears no
date, but from it's place in the letter book was written in 1794.

Sir
    The letter on the other side, to which I have received
no answer.
    I now inform you that the suit will come to trial at
the next district (court) of King and Queen, so that it is
probable judgment will go against me, I wish to be informed
whether you desire that I should go through the superior
courts; if you do, you must furnish me with money for the
purpose. My opinion is that the cause is a bad one, and
that I shall have recourse to you for indemnification. The
land is poor, and will probably be sold. I conceive it will
be prudent in you to make some private bargain with Fog, because I am suspicious I know a person, who will give a liberal
price for it, should it be sold by private auction
    I have sent a letter to the care of the Clerk of the
counties of

LEGAL PAPERS

Beverley to Noel   (continued)

Campbell and Bedford, because I am solicitous you should see them.

                                           I am your obed st
                                              ROBERT BEVERLEY
MR CORNELIUS NOEL   Blandfield   Essex County
   in
Campbell or Bedford
   County

ROBERT BEVERLEY to CORNELIUS NOEL,
2nd March 1794.
Letter Book of ROBERT BEVERLEY (as foregoing)
Letters by date, pages not numbered.

Sir
     The sheriff informed me some days ago that he should soon serve a writ of right upon me for the land I purchased from you in 1773. This land was bequeathed by your grandfather NATHANIEL FOG to your mother, it contains 200 acres, and altho' far from rich, it is nevertheless convenient to me, on it there may be about 25 acres of valuable swamp, part of which is now in meadow.
     At the same time that this writ is to be served upon me, others are to issue against the children of your uncles JOSEPH and THOMAS FOG, and those, who have purchased from them. The plaintiff is JOHN FOG, the son of NATHANIEL FOGs eldest son. Pleas are that the will of NATHANIEL FOG was admitted to record upon the oath of only one witness, and that the bequests were to his children without inserting the word "heirs". The pleas with respec to the record, I believe, may be sufficient, but, I suspect, that the late adjucation of the court of appeals will defeat the other.
     I have embraced the earliest opportunity of communicating this matter to you, that you may come hither, and endeavour to compromise it with the prosecutor, by which you may probably save both expense and trouble. Should the suit go on, it will be determined in 12 months, as the district court of King and Queen has bery little business, and dispatches that little with rapidity.
     I shall in the meantime take such steps as I shall judge best. If you be pleased to write to me, direct your letters to the care of COLONEL ROBERT GAMBLE in Richmond.

                                             I am, sir, V. obed'y
                                             ROBERT BEVERLY
                                             Blandfield, Essex
MR CORNELIUS NOEL   March 2'd 1794
of the county of
   Bedford

LEGAL PAPERS

WEBB TO BEVERLEY

Beverley Family papers.
"Blandfield",
Caret P.O., Essex County, Virginia.

Paper addressed to "ROBERT BEVERLEY Esqr
            Blandfield
             Essex"

ROBERT BEVERLEY Esqr   To JAMES WEBB Dr.

1795 decr	To fee on ms to establish evidence) of NATH'L FOGG's will in Essex ct))	
1796 Jany	To do on mo. th have said will) committed to record)	Ł 1. 10.
1797 March	To fee vs JOSEPH DAY, EDWIN etc ch'y) Essex)	1. 10
1797 Novr	To do on mo, vs SAMUEL TAYLOR on) replevy bond for rent) K & Q	15
		1 2. 45. 0

Sir
    Above is a copy of my acc't against your dec'd father and having occasion at present for as much money as I can collect you will oblige me by paying the acc't as soon as your conscience will admit.

                    With great respect I am, sir,
                         Your very obed't ser't
                              JAMES WEBB

Essex County towit
    JAMES WEBB made oath to the truth of the above acc't and that the same is still justly due. Given under my hand this 16th day of feby 1801.
                    TUNSTALL BANKS

Law'r Muse Esq'r will be pleased to receive for me from Mr Beverley the within mentioned Ł 3.15. as it is in gold and we have no way of weighing it
                         JAMES WEBB
                         Tappa. Sept. 21st 1801

            (continued)

LEGAL PAPERS

Webb to Beverley   (continued)

Tappah'k Sept 21, 1801. Rec'd of MR ROBERT BEVERLEY three
Pounds fifteen shillings on acct of MR JAMES WEBB

                                               ALEX P. MUSE
                                                    for
                                             LAWRENCE MUSE

Note: One does not know whether to laugh or cry in regard to
this account. The very good, the very plain, the very Baptist
Mr. Webb dunning the aristocratic, Episcopalian and very Royalist,
not to say superior Mr. Beverley for the long overdue account.
Mr. Beverley pays immediately in gold, which unfortunately
neither Mr. Webb or any of his associates are able to count.
                                                                 B.F.

* * * * * *

KING AND QUEEN FEES
1794

Archives Division
Virginia State Library,
Richmond, Virginia.

Caroline County. Loose papers. 1794.

King and Queen fees for 94

	1792	1793	1794
MINOR JOHN	15	2.94	
MARTIN TH'S	1.15	1.52	18
DABNEY BENJ	23		
ROWE THO ESTR	1.90		1.16
WYATT HENRY		2.10	3.36
SHACKELFORD LYNE		58	40
GATEWOOD CHAINY			95
FLEET JNO.			95
DEW THOS			3.74
HILL WM & CO.			.60
SPILLER BENJ			1,84
SEGAR RICHD			.54
	3.49	7.14	13.72

                                  (signed) RICHD BROOKE
                                           Sh K & Queen

LEGAL PAPERS

WILL OF ELIZABETH PENDLETON

From the collection of
MR. GEORGE HARRISON SANFORD KING,
1301 Prince Edward St.,
Fredericksburg, Virginia.

Note: Mr. King has also been kind enough to send notations and other papers in connection with this will.   B.F.

In the name of God, Amen: I, ELIZABETH PENDLETON of the County of King and Queen and the State of Virginia, do make and publish this my last will and testament as follows, to Wit:
   Item: I desire that as soon after my death as circumstances permit, that the whole of the Estate both real and personal, to which I am entitled under the will of my brother, JOHN CAMPBELL, dec'd, late of the town of Jackson and the State of Mississippi, be divided among all my children now living in the following manner:
   I give to my daughter JULIANN CARLTON one fifth part of said Estate, to my son WILLIAM H. WOOD one fifth part, to my daughter OLIVIA CARLTON one fifth part, to my son JOHN C. WOOD one fifth part, and to my daughter MARY C. PENDLETON the remaining fifth part, but she is to pay her sister OLIVIA CARLTON the Sum of five hundred dollars out of that portion which she may receive.
   Item: If either of my children above named should die leaving no legal child, then I wish that that portion of my Estate herein devised to him or her, equally divided among the surviving brothers and sisters.
   Lastly, I appoint BENONI CARLTON Executor of This my last will and testament. In witness whereof I have subscribed my name and affixed my seal this 31st day of August 1847.

                         ELIZABETH PENDLETON   (seal)

Signed sealed and acknowledged
Before us
EDWARD S. ACREE
EDWARD CLAYTON
EDWARD R. BOUGHAN

The original of this copy is held by ROLAND ACREE WADDILL who inherited the papers of his grandfather EDWARD SMITH ACREE.
ANN W. FOX

        (see next page for notes)

LEGAL PAPERS

Will of Elizabeth Pendleton   (continued)

Note by G.H.S. King:

This Elizabeth Pendleton was a daughter of Capt. Whitaker Campbell by his 2nd wife Martha Deshazo. See list of children:

Captain Whitaker Campbell and 1st wife Jane Hill had:
1. Lieut. Whitaker Campbell of Gloucester Co.
2. William Campbell of Orange Co.
3. Alexander Campbell of King and Queen Co.
4. Mary (called Polly) mar. Bennoni Carlton Sr.
5. Priscilla mar. Capt. Robert Courtney.
6. Jane mar. - Jones

Capt. Whitaker Campbell and 2nd wife Martha Deshazo had:
7. Peter Campbell - no data -
8. John Campbell (called Jack) died unmarried in Mississippi
9. Elizabeth (called Betsy) mar. 1st James Wood: mar. 2nd Robert Pendleton.
10. Sarah Campbell (called Sally) mar. Robert Courtney Jr. of Richmond, Virginia.

Further note by Mr. Geo. H.S. King: - Robert Courtney Jr. was a nephew of Robert Courtney Sr. (above).
Bennoni Carlton Sr. was a widower when he mar. Mary Campbell, and he had a son by his first wife Bennoni Carlton Jr. who had a daughter John Ella Carlton who married Edward Campbell Fox, son of Edward Fox of King and Queen Co. Bennoni Carlton Sr. may have had other sons also by his 1st wife, and these may have been the husbands of Elizabeth Pendleton's two daughters, mentioned in her will. This is only conjecture of course, but note the many intermarriages.
I have corresponded with Capt. A.C. Jones of Three Creeks, Arkansas who is directly descended from Jane Campbell, 6th child of Captain Whitaker Campbell.
We have never before had a list of Elizabeth Pendleton's children. I do not understand why she had no estate from either husband to will, only the estate left her by her brother. Neither do I know who Edward Clayton was, unless he was father of Peter Clayton who married Elizabeth Fox. Note that James Robert Clayton was half brother to Enoch and Pike Clayton.

See next page for a/c of estate of
PIKE M. CLAYTON

LEGAL PAPERS

Will of Elizabeth Pendleton (continued)
Mr. Geo. H.S. King's notes.

The Estate of Pike M. Clayton, desc'd
In account with Enoch M. Clayton Administrator

Dr
1854 Feb. 13		To paid tax on administration	75.
	24	To paid B. Carlton, Thos Haynes and Edward C. Fox $1.00 each for services as appraisers	3.00
		To paid Enoch M. Clayton (on 13th inst) balance due from Intestate to him on purchase of negro boy Roy sold to him by Intestate in his lifetime	377.22
		To paid Peter Toomly for auctioneering Estate	1.00
		To paid for clothes for boy Roy previous to sale	1.95
		To paid N.B. and C.B. Hill for express on decedents trunk from Mobile	7.25
1855 Feb. 13		To paid J.H.C. Jones for motions for qualification, appointment of appraisers etc	5.00
		To retained to pay for stating and recording this account	4.50
		To commission 5% on 655.00	32.75
			- - - -
			221.58
			433.42
			- - - -
			655.00

Cr.
1854 Feb. 13		By this sum of George M. Pendleton for purchase of negro boy Roy belonging to Intestate	595.00
	Aug. 13	By E.M. Clayton for gold watch	60.00
			- - - -
			655.00

For distribution of estate see next page.

LEGAL PAPERS

Will of Elizabeth Pendleton (continued)
Mr. Geo H.S. King's notes.

Distribution of Estate of Pike M. Clayton

```
1855 Feb. 13    Balance due Estate this day to debit    221.58
     Aug. 13    Interest thereon to date                  6.64
                                                        - - - -
                                                        228.22
```

Distributable as follows, to wit:

```
To Enoch M. Clayton whole brother              50.71 5/9
To Mary E. Dix whole sister                    50.71 5/9
To James Ro: Clayton, half brother             25.35.7/9
To Thos. S. Butler, half brother               25.35 7/9
To Jos. H. Butler, half brother                25.35 7/9
To Samuel Butler, in right of his dec'd wife
     Elizabeth who was the Intestate's mother  50.71 5/9
                                              - - - - -
                                               228.22
```

* * * * * *

COURTNEY INSCRIPTIONS

Hollywood Cemetary, Richmond, Virginia.
Section of Dr. R.A. PATTERSON of "Reveille" in the old part of the cemetary, near the Confederate section.

In memory of
SARAH
wife of
ROBT. COURTNEY
of Henrico
and Daughter of
Capt Whitaker Campbell
of King and Queen
Born Nov. 2, 1795
Died
March 29, 1860

See next page

Courtney Inscriptions (continued)

>Sacred
>to the memory of
>ROBERT COURTNEY
>Died
>September 3rd 1861
>in the 75th year of his age.

* * * * * *

CRAIG's JUDGEMENT
1789

Family papers of JUDGE FRANCIS WYATT SMITH,
"Smithfield", King and Queen County, Virginia.
Particularly the papers of JAMES WEBB, Attorney.

Marked: Memo of Craigs Judgt
                vs Richards Shff of K & Q.

                to carry to the dist court

                soire facias ordered in
                K & Qu Ct.

On Tuesday the 11th of August 1789 A CRAIG by JO CATLETT his atty moved the court of Kg & Queen county, and obtained a judgmt (agst) WILLIAM RICHARDS Gent late Shrff etc for 861 lbs of Tobo the balance due on the sd Richards Recep't for fees put into his hands to collect and due to the said Craig and also for his costs etc - - - -to be discharged by the paya't of 12/16 pr Ct Costs of Judgt
Clks fees   57 lb Tobo
Attys fee 15/or 150

WILLIAM RICHARDS is dead
THOS RICHARDS is his Exor
No Ex'on issued

LEGAL PAPERS

WILL OF THACKER MUIRE

Records of King and Queen County,
King and Queen C.H., Virginia.

In the name of God Amen   I THACKER MUIRE of Walkerton in King and Queen County being in perfect health and of sound and disposing mind and memory do make and ordain this my last Will and Testament in manner and form following to wit

Item the 1" It is my will and desire that all my just debts and funeral expenses be paid

Item the 2" It is my will and desire that should my executrix and executors herein after named upon consultation and advisement together after my death, consider it most expedient and conductive to the interest of my family that my tract of land called "Greenbrier" containing Five hundred and twenty one and a half acres lying in the County of King and Queen adjoining the lands of JOSIAH RYLAND   JOHN WALKER and A.G. SALE, be sold, they shall have power to do so, on the best terms and on such credit as they may deem most judicious.

Item 3d After the satisfaction of my just debts and funeral expenses, I then lend to my dear well beloved wife, SARAH ANN MUIRE, the whole of my estate real and personal and mixed of every kind and description to be under her entire control and management so long as she continues my widow. Should she marry again, then I desire that she take one third of my whole estate which I loan to her as long as she may live and at her death the said third part thus taken I give and bequeath to my son THOMAS LOGAN DOUGLASS MUIRE to him and his heirs forever.

Item 4th At the marriage of my wife, should she marry again, the remaining two thirds of the whole of my estate I give and bequeath to my said son THOMAS LOGAN DOUGLASS MUIRE to him and his heirs forever.

Item 5th Should my said wife have other issue lawfully begotten by me, then I desire that the whole of my estate subject to the provision made for my wife SARAH ANN MUIRE may be equally divided among them both.

Item 6th I am entitled to an undivided interest in a parcel of negroes by virtue of my second marriage with MARIA MEACHAM THORNTON, these negroes are now in possession of MRS. ELIZABETH L. TALIAFERRO of Gloucester County, who is the sister of my wife MARIA M. MUIRE. MRS. GEORGE formerly of the County of Middlesex, the grand mother of ELIZABETH LEE HACKNEY (now E.L. Taliaferro) MARIA MEACHAM HACKNEY

LEGAL PAPERS

Will of Thacker Muire   (continued)

and NANCY HACKNEY left to her grand daughter E.L. HACKNEY (now E.L. Taliaferro) as long as she lived, a negro girl (I think named Lucinda) and her increase. At the death of the said E.L. Taliaferro the said girl and her increase are to be equally divided between MARIA MEACHAM my late wife, and her sister NANCY the sisters of the said ELIZABETH L. TALIAFERRO and the grand daughters of Mrs George - So my wife informed me. Which undivided interest whenever it falls in I loan to my wife SARAH ANN MUIRE during her widowhood or natural life and at her death or marriage I give the same to be divided in the same manner mentioned in the fourth and fifth clauses of this Will

Item the 7th   It is my wish and desire that my son THOMAS LOGAN DOUGLASS MUIRE, shall be educated in the best manner consistly with the means of my Estate, and recommend for this purpose, that he be sent to Randolph Macon College, but should my said son die during his minority, unmarried, and without issue then I give and bequeath all my estate of every description whatsoever to my dear wife SARAH ANN MUIRE as long as she lives and at her death I desire that one half of what she may leave be divided amongst my wife's relations and the other half between my Brother's daughter CATHERINE W. MUIRE and the children of my Sister ELIZABETH SHEPPARD.

Item the 8th   If it should be found practicable to pay all my just debts by the sale of my land and other property herein authorized to be sold without submitting to a sacrifice of my landed estate I desire that none of my Slaves shall be sold for that purpose But if any of them should become unmanageable at any time or if a fair price cannot be obtained for the Land mentioned above my executrix and executors hereinafter named may have the power to dispose of any of them either by private sale or public auction in the City of Richmond as to them may seem best having regard as well to the future happiness of such as it may be found necessary to sell, as to the interest of my Estate.

Item the 9th   I do not wish my Land and Ferry at this place sold but if my Executrix and Executors shall consider it best for the interest of my family to do so, then I give them power to sell it upon the same terms mentioned with reference to my "Greenbriar" tract adjoining JOSIAH RYLAND and others.

Item the 10th   If my Land and ferry at this place be sold I desire that my tract containing One hundred acres called "Shady Grove" near this place be sold at the same time and upon the same terms.

LEGAL PAPERS

Will of Thacker Muire (continued)

Item the 11th I desire that no inventory and Appraisement of my estate be made and that there be no publick sale of my perishable property but such part thereof as my dear wife can conveniently spare may be disposed of my my Executrix and Executors hereinafter named by private sale on such terms as to them shall seem best.

Item the 12th I constitute and appoint my beloved wife SARAH ANN MUIRE my Executrix and my friends FRANCIS W. SCOTT, DOCT DANIEL H. GREGG and SAMUEL F. HARWOOD Executors of this my last Will and Testament and request that no security be required of my Executrix

Given under my hand and seal this 8th day of February eighteen hundred and forty nine

                                    THACKER MUIRE   (seal

Signed sealed published and
declared by THACKER MUIRE
to be his last Will and Testament
and signed by us as witnesses
at his request

    YOUNG I. CLEMENTS
    ELIZA R. CLEMENTS

CODICILE

As the wind and weather of shifts and changes, so men like the weather, often change in their friendship according to circumstances and from the most profound and warm possessions of friendship and attachment, become cold and indifferent to their old friends without assigning any reason for the change. So in like manner some of my Exors named in this my last Will and Testament may change in their friendship and say I wont qualify to the Will: To release them of the pain or pleasure of so doing I hereby nominate and appoint my beloved wife SARAH ANN MUIRE my Exex and my friend DOCT D.H. GREGG my Exor and them only, until my son THOMAS LOGAN DOUGLASS MUIRE becomes of lawful age. Then and in that case I desire him to qualify and act jointly as my Exor with my beloved wife and my friend Doct DANIEL H. GREGG until my estate is fully settled up, and none else requesting the Court to require no security of my wife or son

    Given under my hand this 31st day of December 1856
                      THACKER MUIRE   (seal)
At a Quarterly Court held for King and Queen County at Paces Chapel on Thursday the 1st day of December 1866
This last will and Testament of THACKER MUIRE deceased and the Codicil annexed was offered for proof by SARAH ANN MUIRE the Executrix therein named and J.H.C. JONES and ROBERT POLLARD JR. were

LEGAL PAPERS

Will of Thacker Muire (continued)

sworn and severally deposed that they were well acquainted with the Testators handwriting and verily believed that the said writing and Codicil annexed and the name thereto subscribed to be wholly written by the Testators own hand. Whereupon the said writing is ordered to be recorded as the true Will and Testament of the said THACKER MUIRE deceased

                              Teste
                                    ROBERT POLLARD J CC

                          Truly recorded
                                        Teste

Note: Thacker Muir died just prior to 25th July 1863. This deformed eccentric was 83 years of age. The word in the Fleet family was that he knew just enough of religion and law to make mischief for anyone he came in contact with. He was married three times. The foregoing will, evidently written by himself, is by no means the effort of a fool. In fact there would be no indication that he was in any way abnormal but for the codicil, and that, with it's swift shot of truth at Francis W. Scott and Samuel F. Harwood makes us wonder if he did not know more than our ancestors thought?   B.F.

                        * * * * * *

                      BEVERLEY TO ELLIOTT

Letter Book of ROBERT BEVERLEY of "Blandfield". 1790-1821. Now (1942) belonging to BLAND BEVERLEY, Esq., of "Blandfield", Essex County, Virginia.

MR WILLIAM ELLIOTT
     Take notice you must leave the tenement you now live upon at the end of this year, one thousand eight hundred and one.
                              ROBERT BEVERLEY

Blandfield, May 7th 1801

This notice was delivered by THOMAS LUMPKIN.

LEGAL PAPERS

JUSTICES
1799 - 1801

Archives Division.
Virginia State Library, Richmond, Virginia.
Executive Papers. JAMES MONROE, Governor.
August 1801.

At a quarterly Court held for King and Queen County at the Courthouse on Monday the 10th of August 1801
It is ordered that the Clerk of this Court do certify to the Executive of this Commonwealth that ANDERSON SCOTT, WILLIAM DUDLEY, LARKIN SMITH, ANTHONY GARDNER, RICHARD BROOKE, THOMAS C. MARTIN, JOHN WEDDERBURN, JOHN HOSKINS, HUMPHREY WALKER, HENRY YOUNG, SAMUEL G. FAUNTLEROY, ROBERT HOSKINS, BEVERLY ROY, RICHARD CORBIN, THOMAS ROANE jun'r, ROBERT B. SEMPLE, ROBERT B. HILL, BENJAMIN HOOMES and WILLIAM TEMPLE Gentlemen are the present acting Justices of the peace for this County, that PHILIP PENDLETON, Gent'n is Sheriff and that the Clerk do also certify the days that each Magistrate has set in Court the two last years past

                              Teste

                                   RO: POLLARD C.C.

Agreeable to the foregoing Order I do hereby certify that I have examined the proceedings of the County Court of King and Queen and find that the Magistrates were present on the Court days under their respective names affixed

               ANDERSON SCOTT
                  11th May 1801
                  12th May

               WILLIAM DUDLEY
                  1799 Augt 13th
                       14th
                       15th
                  Septr 9th
                  Novr 13th

                  (continued)

LEGAL PAPERS

Justices.   1799 - 1801 (continued)

        LARKIN SMITH
          1799 August 12th
                    13th
             Nov'r 11th
                    14th
                    15th
          1800 March 13th
                    14th
             April 14th
               May 12th
                    15th
              July 14th
              Sept 18th
              Novr 10th

          1801 Feby 9th
              March 9th
                    12th
             April 13th
             July 13th

        WILLIAM FLEET
          1799 Augt 12th

        ANTHONY GARDNER
          1800 October 13th
          1801 Jany 12th
              May 11th

        RICH'd BROOKE
          1799 Augt 12th
                    13th
                    14th
             Novr 11th
                    12th
                    13th
                    14th
          1800 Jany 13th
              Feb 10th
             March 10th
                    11th
                    14th
             April 14th

LEGAL PAPERS

Justices, 1799 - 1801 (continued)

            RICH'D BROOKE
        1800 May 12th
               13th
           Aug't 11th
               12th
               13th
           Octr 13th
           Dec 8th
               9th

       1801 March 11th
               12th
          April 13th
           June 18th

          THOMAS C. MARTIN
      1799 Aug't 12th
         Nov'r 13th
              14th
              15th
          Dec'r 9th
      1800 May 12th
              13th
      1801 Jany 12th
         April 13th
         June 8th
         July 13th

          PHILIP PENDLETON
      1799 Sept 9th
              10th
      1800 March 10th
              11th
              12th
              13th
         April 14th
         June 9th
         July 15th
        Aug't 13th
              14th
         Dec'r 8th
               9th

(continued)

LEGAL PAPERS

Justices 1799 - 1801. (continued)

JOHN WEDDERBURN
(blank - no dates of attendance shown)

JOHN HOSKINS
1799 Aug't 12th
     Sep'r 9th
     Novr 11th
     Decr   9th
1800 Jany 13th
     March 10th
           11th
           12th
     April 14th
     May   12th
     July 14th
           15th
     Augt 11th
           12th
           14th
     Sep'r 8th
     Nov'r 10th
     Decr   8th
1801 Jany 12th
     Feby   9th
     March 9th
            10th
            11th
     June   8th
     July 13th

RICH'd CORBIN
(blank - no dates of attendance shown)

JOHN KIDD
1799 Aug't 12th
           13th
           14th
           15th
     Septr 9th
            10th
     Novr 14th
           15th
           16th

LEGAL PAPERS

Justices 1799 - 1801 (continued)

```
                THO'S ROANE JR
                  1799 Aug't 12th
                             13th
                             14th
                       Sept  9th
                             10th
                  1800 March 11th
                             12th
                       May  15th
                       July 14th
                             15th
                       Augt 14th
                       Sept  8th
                  1801 Feby  9th
                       March 9th
                             10th
                             11th
                             12th
                       July 13th


              ROBERT B. SEMPLE
                  1799 Augt 14th
                            15th
                       Novr 11th
                            15th
                            16th
                  1800 Feby 10th
                       March 10th
                             13th
                             14th
                       Augt 11th
                  1801 Jany 12th
                       March 11th
                             12th


              ROBERT B. HILL
                  1799 Dec'r  9th
                  1800 March 10th
                       April 14th
                       May  12th
                            13th
                            14th
                            15th
```

(continued)

90

LEGAL PAPERS

Justices 1799 - 1801 (continued)

ROBERT B. HILL
1800 June 9th
July 15th
Augt 13th
14th
Nov'r 10th
Dec'r 18th
1801 Jany 12th
March 9th
12th
April 13th
May 11th
12th
June 18th

HUMPHREY WALKER
1799 Augt 12th
14th
15th
Septr 10th
Nov'r 13th
14th
1800 Jany 13th
March 10th
12th
13th
14th
May 12th
13th
July 14th
15th
Augt 13th
Sept 8th
Decr 8th
1801 Feby 9th
March 9th
10th
11th
April 13th
May 12th
July 13th

(continued)

LEGAL PAPERS

Justices 1799 - 1801   (continued)

    HENRY YOUNG
     1799 Septr 9th
     1800 Jany 13th
       May 12th
       Augt 11th

    SAML G. FAUNTLEROY
     1799 Dec'r 9th
     1800 Augt 11th
       12th
      Oct 13th
     1801 March 9th
       10th
       11th
      April 13th
      July 13th

    ROBERT HOSKINS
     1799 Nov'r 15th
     1800 Feby 10th
       May 12th
        15th
      June 9th
      Augt 13th
      Septr 8th
      Octr 13th
      Novr 10th
     1801 May 11th
       12th
      June 8th

    BEVERLEY ROY (Note: this name usually
     1799 Sept.9th spelled Beverly Roy.
      Novr 13th   B.F.)
       14th
       16th
     1800 Jany 13th
      May 12th
       15th
     1801 May 11th
       12th
      June 8th

LEGAL PAPERS

Justices 1799 - 1801. (continued)

BENJAMIN HOOMES
1799 Aug't 14th
         15th
     Septr 9th
           10th
     Novr 11th
          15th
          16th
1800 Feby 10th
     March 14th
     April 14th
     May 12th
         13th
     June 9th
     Augt 11th
          13th
     Septr 8th
     Octr 13th
     Novr 10th
     Decr 9th
1801 Feby 9th
     March 12th
     May 11th

WILLIAM TEMPLE
1799 Sept 9th
     Decr 9th
1800 March 10th
           11th
           12th
     April 14th
     May 12th
     July 14th
     Augt 12th
     Septr 8th
     Decr 8th
1801 July 13th

RO. POLLARD C.C.

LEGAL PAPERS

ROBINSON TO CHURCHILL

Manuscript Division,
Duke University,
Durham, NC.

Benville 27th Apl. 1801

Dear Sir
    When I was down here before, and had returned from Middlesex, I put into Mr Dabney's hands my Acco't against you for sundry claims proposing to him to effect an amicable settlement with you in the first place; I hope you will therefore name to him some short period, and give your note to that Effect.
    The settlement of my Bro'r Ch: Estate is about to be made, and I will take upon myself this unfinished part very cheerfully if you will give me your Bond or Note, payable at a short Date, for the amount.
    I trust when you view the steps I am now taking to finish the collection you will also take into consideration the different attempts I have made to meet you, for an adjustment. The solicitations to make it through the medium of MR WM ROBINSON who knows every circumstance of the Transactions between us. All these proving ineffectual, I hope you will take this last step of using the agency of Mr. Dabney, in good part, and if not settle it with him before his return from Court, that you will come to Benville in the course of this week, where we shall be all extremely happy to see you. Your Sister and Nieces and Benja beg me to present their Love and respects to you with great wishes to see you

                  I am with respect
                  Dr Sir y'r sincere F and hbl
                        serv't

                  NEEDLER ROBINSON

P.S.
    If you should see MR WM ROBINSON pray inform him he has been expected here and I should be glad if he will accompany you down.   N.R.

Addressed to:
            THOS. E. CHURCHILL Esqr
                Middlesex
            hon'rd by
            B. DABNEY Esq

LEGAL PAPERS

SCOTT TO WEBB
Accounts 1798

Family papers of JUDGE FRANCIS WYATT SMITH, "Smithfield", King and Queen County, Va. Particularly the papers of JAMES WEBB, Attorney.

List Marked:

Rec't
John Scott agent
for Jas Ritchie & Co
on bonds returned
Nov'r 98

List signed "JOHN SCOTT, Tappahannock, 20th Novr 1798, Bonds etc for Mr Webb"
Three sheets headed "dates of Bonds, sums due, Debtors, their Residence and Remarks"

The list includes:

1773 Octr 16   Bond dem'd 45. 13. 7 1/2 JAMES BATES, living in King and Queen he owes a small open acc't also

1771 Nov 18   Bond 28 May 1772 Ł 8. 2. 6 CALEB BOULWARE and YOUNGER PITTS. Enquire for these persons or their Representatives before Suit is bro't.

(No date here) Bond bal due 2 Apl 77. JOHN CORRIE dec'd. B. ROY and THAD: WILLIAMS Exors. Suit to be bro't for the benefit of J R & Co

1776 Feby 5   Bond dem'd Ł 12. 0. 11 THOMAS FALCONER chair maker of Kg and Queen (sued)

(No date here) Signed acc't 25. 4. 10 1/2 GEO GREEN dec'd Writ against ROBT BAYLOR and WM WARING junr Exr of SIMON MILLER who was Exr of GEO GREEN (sued)

1771 Apl 3   Bond due 3 Nov 1771 4. 17. 5 EDW'D GOULDMAN and ROBT PARKER. JOHN PARKER of Kg & Queen Exr of R. PARKER (sued)

1774 Apl 14   Bond Ł 10. 18 MAJOR LAFONN. JOSEPH BOHANNON Exr (sued)

1776 Feb 6   Bond 35. 8. 9 open acct 18. 4 DAVID PITTS junr King & Queen: I believe he is dead. Enquire for his Representatives.

(continued)

LEGAL PAPERS

Scott to Webb (continued)

1775 Feby 3   Bond due 28 July '75. 12. 3. 5 THOMAS BOULWARE.
              His son OBADIAH BOULWARE Ex'r.

              JOSEPH PURKS account returned
              EDMUND SPEARMAN account returned

* * * * * *

SEGAR VS SAMUEL
1796

Archives Division,
Virginia State Library,
Richmond, Virginia.
Caroline County Suits.

Note: This suit appears to have been a petty quarrel that dragged through the Caroline County courts from 1796 to 1800. It all seems to have been over the use of a still. RICHARD SEGAR states that ACHILLES DULING stirred up the trouble in the first place. The papers are valueless other than showing that such persons (Alas! of small vision and scope) lived at such a time and place. THOMAS C. MARTIN and PHILIP PENDLETON were Justices of the Peace in King and Queen, according to these papers, on 8 May 1800.

RICHARD SEGAR plt.
GRAY SAMUEL Deft.

MR GRAY SAMUEL
    Sir Please to take notice that on friday 23rd Inst at Mr Turners Tavern in the Town of Dunkirk I shall proceed to take the deposition of MR JOHN SCHOOLS in a suit depending in the Cot'y Court of Caroline between my self plt and yourself Deft You may attend if you think proper.

                              I am yrs etc
                                R. SEGAR
May 14, 1800

King and Queen to wit
    JOHN SEGAR jun'r made oath before me that he delivered a true copy of the with (within) to GRAY SAMUEL on the 14th May 1800. Given under my hand this 23d of the same month in the year aforesaid
                         THO'S C. MARTIN

LEGAL PAPERS

Segar vs Samuel (continued)

RICHARD SEGAR Plt)
GRAY SAMUEL Dft   )

    The deposition of JOHN SCHOOLS of lawful age deposeth and saith x x x at the time the suite was tryed while ACHILLES DULING was given in his evidence RICH'D SEGAR spoke to him in an offencive manner x x x Ques (by Plt) is not Mr Duling a near neighbour to you A. he is x x x x Question by the Deft. did not Mr Duling at the time of geting mad make mention of Mr Segars charging him with being in a secret plot with MERIDA BATES and myself at his house in order to extort words from him. Answer, that was mention amongst the rest of the Conversation question, was not that charge proved to be fals by the Evidence of Mr Bates Answer I am not certain but I believe it was. and further this deponent saith not

JOHN SCHOOLS

Caroline County August 9th 1799 this deposition of JOHN SCHOOLS he being first sworn was this day taken before me in presents of the Plt and Deft

REUBEN CHAPMAN

RICHARD SEGAR Plt)
GRAY SAMUEL Deft   )

    The deposition of GILES RICHERSON of lawful age being first sworn deposeth and saith, that at the time when ACHILLES DULING was given in his Evidence he appeared to be warm but he this deponent thought it was on account of Mr Segars enterrupt'g him question by the Deft. did it appear to you that Mr Duling was partial in favor of Mr Samuel
    Answer I did not discover any partiality; but I thought Mr Duling gave in his Evidence with a good deal of freedom and further this deponant saith not

GILES RICHESON

Caroline County Augt 9th 1799 this deposition of GILES RICHERSON he being first sworn was this day taken befoer me in the presents of the Plt and Deft.

REUBEN CHAPMAN

Caroline October Court 1796
Ordered that GRAY SAMUEL pay ACHILLES DULING Twenty three Dollars and Sixty four Cents for attending Court twelve days and travelling to and from the said Court Two hundred and sixteen miles as a witness for him against RICHARD SEGAR
                      A Copy   JNO. PENDLETON.

LEGAL PAPERS

Segar vs Samuel (continued)

RICHARD SEGAR Plt)
  against)
GRAY SAMUEL Dft)

The deposition of JOHN SCHOOLS of lawful age taken and sworn to at Mr Turners Tavern in the Town of Dunkirk on friday 23rd May deposeth and saith. That while this suit was depending I was frequently in company with ACHILLES DULING that he was always endeavouring to supplant my judgment as it appeared to me in order to weaken my opinion and to establish his as witness in said suit

Qu
How much brandy do you think I lost in consequence of Mr Samuels disappointing me in the still the wobley stands which he made for me leaking out the Liquor

Ans'r
According to what I saw I think you must have lost twenty Gallons

                              JOHN SCHOOLS

King and Queen to wit
JOHN SCHOOLS personally appeared before us and made oath to the truth of the above. Given under our hands this 28th day of May 1800

                              THOS. C. MARTIN
                              PHILIP PENDLETON

* * * * * *

SADLER TO WEBB

Family papers of JUDGE FRANCIS WYATT SMITH, "Smithfield", King and Queen County, Va. Particularly the papers of JAMES WEBB, Atty.

Dear Sir
    the witnesses that I want summoned between MARGET CLARKs Exutors and ELISABETH BROOKEs Exutors is THOMAS GREENWOOD and MARGAT GREENWOOD his wife

                              JOHN SADLER

Mr   the 20 of Janary 1800
JAMES WEBB

LEGAL PAPERS

MANN VS HARWOOD JR

Family papers of JUDGE FRANCIS WYATT SMITH, "Smithfield", King and Queen County, Virginia. Particularly the papers of JAMES WEBB, Attorney

Endorsed: Mann   )
                   vs   )   Jud't
                   Harwood jr   )

At a superior Court for the District composed of the Counties of Essex, Middlesex, King and Queen and King William, held at King and Queen Courthouse the 21st day of April 1795

```
         ROBERT MANN                      plt    )
            against                              )
         JOHN HARWOOD junr survivor              )    In Debt
         of CHRISTOPHER HARWOOD and              )
         JOHN HARWOOD jr                  Deft   )
```

This day came the parties by their attorneys, and thereupon came also a Jury, to wit, ROBERT SMITH, CHARLES WILLIAMS, WILLIAM MONTAGUE, ROBERT HOSKINS, JOHN RICHARDS, WILSON ROWE, ROBERT SMITH junr, WILLIAM BIRD, BENONI CARLTON, THOMAS JOHNSON, MERIWETHER SKELTON, and RICHARD BAGBY, who being elected, tried and sworn well and truly to try the issue joined, upon their Oaths to say, that the Defendant hath not paid to the plaintiff the Debt in the Declaration mentioned as the plaintiff by replying hath alledged, and they do assess the Damages of the said plaintiff by occasion of the detention of the said Debt to one penny. Therefore it is considered by the Court that the plaintiff recover against the Defendant the sum of Two hundred pounds Current Gold or Silver coin at their value, the Debt in the Declaration mentioned, together with his Damages aforesaid in form aforesaid assessed, and also his Costs in this behalf expended and the said Defendant in money etc
But this Judgement is to be discharged by the payment of One hundred pounds Current Gold or Silver, with Interest thereon, to be computed after the rate of five per centum per annum, from the fourteenth Day of October One thousand seven hundred and ninety two till paid and the Damages and Costs.

D.C.   A Copy
Costs 9.05   Test
                             RO POLLARD   C.D.C.

LEGAL PAPERS

DUNLOP AND HENDERSON TO DUNLOP AND PENDLETON

Manuscript Division, Duke University.
Durham, North Carolina
The original has mistakenly been placed
in the Rutherfoord Collection at Duke.
It is actually from the papers of JAMES
WEBB, Attorney of "Smithfield" King and
Queen County, Virginia.

Know all men by these presents that I SARAH THACKER DUNLOP otherwise HENDERSON spouse of JAMES ELLIOTT HENDERSON of the city of Glasgow in the county of Lanark in that part of Great Britain called Scotland merchant, and I the said JAMES ELIOT HENDERSON for myself and my interest and as taking full burden upon me for my said wife, have and each of us hath made named constituted and appointed x x x WILLIAM DUNLOP merchant in Port Royal and EDMUND PENDLETON Junior attorney both of Caroline County Virginia Esquires to be our true and lawful attornies x x to settle x x the afairs and estate of the deceased SARAH THACKER late of King and Queen County in Virginia North America some time wife of LEONARD HILL thereafter of JAMES CAMPBELL in the County of Essex in Virginia aforesaid all now deceased x x x x In witness whereof we have hereunto set our hands and seals at the Hill of Ardmore near the Town of Dumbarton in Scotland the Thirtieth day of July in the year of our Lord seventeen hundred and ninety eight

Wit:
L H DUNLOP
DAVID ALLAN yst (youngest)

signed SARAH THACKER DUNLOP
          JAS. E. HENDERSON

LEONARD HILL DUNLOP of the Island of Saint Vincent merchant, at present in Glasgow x x attests to above signatures.

Endorsed:
     May 29th 1812 By virtue of the within rec'd from JAMES WEBB the sum of one hundred and seventy one pounds nineteen shillings and three pence for the legacy of MRS SARAH CAMPBELL dec'd to the within-named SARAH THACKER DUNLOP
                            WM DUNLOP

Test
CHRISTOPHER B. FLEET

LEGAL PAPERS

JAMES WEBB. EXPENSE TO WILLIAMSBURG

Family papers of JUDGE FRANCIS WYATT SMITH, "Smithfield", King and Queen County, Virginia Particularly the papers of JAMES WEBB, Attorney.

Memo of exp's of self, ser't and 2 horses going to, and from Wmsburg

1802		
Oct: 12	pd ferriage at Frazers	₺ -. 3. -
	do at Pannells	-. 4. 6
	exp at New Kent court house)	
	got there at night not having)	
	dined)	-. 9. 9
13	breakfasted and fed horses)	
	at Geddys)	-. 6.10 1/2
	Got to Wmsburg to dinner and)	
	returned from thence in the)	
	morning of the 15th, paid)	
	exp's in Wmsburg)	2. 2. 7 1/2
15	breakfasted and fed horses at)	
	Geddy's)	6. 4
	pd ferriage from Brick house)	
	to West point)	4. 6
	grog at West point)	-. 0. 9
	dinner, horse feeding and)	
	ferriage at Frazers)	-.10. -
	horse feeding 1 night at)	
	Kg and Qu court house)	-. 4. -
		₺ 4.12. 4

* * * * * *

NOMINATION OF SHERIFF

Archives Division.
Virginia State Library, Richmond, Va.
Executive Papers. 1802. Aug. 1st to Nov. 27th.

At a court held for King and Queen county at the courthouse on Monday the 13th of September 1802
The court doth nominate to his excellency JAMES MONROE esquire Governor or chief Magistrate of this Commonwealth, JOHN HOSKINS, HENRY YOUNG and HUMPHREY WALKER Gentlemen as fit and proper persons for one of them to be commissioned Sheriff of this county

                         Test   RO. POLLARD   C.C.

LEGAL PAPERS

WAREHOUSE INSPECTORS

Archives Division,
Virginia State Library,
Richmond, Virginia.
Executive Papers, 1802. Aug. 1st to Nov. 27th.

At a Quarterly court held for King and Queen county at the courthouse on Monday the 8th of November 1802
The court doth recommend unto his excellency JAMES MONROE esquire JOSEPH COLLIER, THOMAS METCALF, JOHN CAMPBELL and ZACHARIAH CRITTENDEN as fit and able persons to be commissioned inspectors of tobacco at Shepherds Warehouse within this county. RICHARD BAGBY and JOHN WATTS as fit and able persons to be commissioned Inspectors of tobacco at Mantapike Warehouse and GABRIEL DIX and WILLIAM GATEWOOD as fit and able persons to be commissioned Inspectors of tobacco at Todds Warehouse within this county

                                        A copy
                                        Teste
                                        WILLIAM TODD   D.C.C.

Endorsed:
                        King and Queen
                         recommendation
                      Inspectors tobacco
                      all in commission
                           at present
                        continued 27th
                           Nov'r 1802

* * * * * * * *

INDEX

A

Abrahams,
  Capt. 35
Acree,
  Edwd. Smith 77
  Wm. 65
Alexander,
  Lt. John 65
Allen,
  David 99
Andrews,
  Thos. P. 65
Armistead,
  Major Thos. 12,13,14,15,16,36
Arnold,
  Genl. Benedict 14,16,42
  Latham 71
Aylett's Warehouse 51

B

Bacon's Ordinary 35
Bagby,
  Lt. John 59,60
  Richd. 98,101
Baldock,
  Richd. 3,5,9
Bagby,
  Capt. Thos. 57,58
Ball,
  Archibald 65
Banks,
  Tunstall 75
Bartlett,
  John 63
Barton,
  William 9
Bates,
  James 95
  Merida 97
Baylor,
  Robt. 95
  Capt. Thos. 24
Baytop,
  Capt. Thos. 25,27
Beazely,
  Gowan 5
Beadles,
  Edmund 38
Bedinger,
  Danl. 13
"Benville" 94
Beverley,
  Bland 74
  Robert 73,74,75,76,85
Birch,
  Vincent 65
Bird,
  Capt. Philemon 59
  Sam 34
  William 98
Blake,
  Benj. R. 26,27
Bland,
  Ensign John Jr. 61
  Richard 65
  Capt. Robert 23
"Blandfield", 73,74,75,85
Bohannon,
  Joseph 95
Bosher,
  Mrs. Ann 25,28
Boughan,
  Edw. R. 77
Boulware,
  Caleb 95
  Obadiah 96
  Thos. 96
Bowler's P.O., 23

Boyd,
  John 59
  Lt. Robt. 59,60,61
  William 59,60
Braxton,
  Hon. Carter 48
Brick House, 100
Brooke,
  Eliza 97
  Col. George 50,51,52,53
  Richard 76,86,87
  William S. 31
Brooking,
  Col. Vivion 52
Brown,
  Archie 65
Brumfield,
  Robt. 35,36,37
  William 36
Brushwood,
  Elijah 63
  James 63
Bullman,
  Thomas 63
Burgess,
  Rd. 27
Burke,
  Robt. 27
Burruss,
  Frances 33
  George 33
  Richd D. 33
Burton,
  Campbell 63
  Elias 63
Burwell,
  Hon. Lewis 1
Burwell's Mill 35,37
Butler,
  David 30,31,32
  Mrs. Eliz 80
  Joseph H. 80
  Saml. 80
  Thos. S. 80
Butler's Oldfields, 31

C

Campbell,
  Alex 78
  James 99
  James and Co. 52
  Jane 78
  Mrs. Jane Hill 78
  John 77,78,101
  Mrs. Martha 78
  Mary (Mrs. Carlton) 78
  Peter 78
  Priscilla 78
  Sarah 78,80,99
  Capt. Whitaker 51,78,80
  William (Orange Co) 78
Carlton,
  Benoni 60,61,77,78,79,98
  Bennoni Jr. 78
  Ellis 64
  John Ella 78
  Juliann 77
  Mary 78
  Olivia 77
Carrington,
  Ed. 25
Carson,
  James 6
  Judge John 18

Catlett,
  Jo 81
Chamberlayne,
  John 65
Chapman,
  Reuben 97
Cheen, (Chinn or Cheek?)
  Eldred 29
Chick,
  James 7
Christian,
  William 34
Churchill,
  Thos. E. 94
Clarke,
  Edwd. 33
  Edmond 33
  George 32
  Henry 63
  Margaret 97
Clayton,
  Edwd. 77,78
  Enoch M. 78,79,80
  Jas. Ro. 80
  Peter 78
  Pike M. 78,79,80
Clements,
  Eliza H. 84
  J. 28
  Young I. 84
Cocke,
  Isaac 36,37
  Capt. Thos. 6
  William 33
Cole,
  John 5,9
Coleman,
  Saml. 14
  Thos. 53
Collier,
  Capt. Charles 19,63
  Joseph 101
Collins,
  Achilles 9
  Lt. Thos 59
  Zachariah 65
Collis,
  Killis 5
Conway,
  John M. 27
Cooke,
  Capt. Dawson 59,61
  Henry 65
Corbin,
  John Tayloe 40,53
  Richard 86,89
  Ensign Richd (1797) 60
  Lieu. Richd (1799) 61
  Capt. Richd. 62
  Richd. Jr. 39,40,41,42,43
  Richd. Jr. (Imprisoned for debt in England) 39
  Richard, Sr. 39,40,41,42,43,44,53
  Robt. B. 29
Corgin Royalists in England 39
Cornwallis,
  Lord 17
Corr,
  James 63
  Sterling 63
Corrie,
  John 95
Courtney,
  Priscilla 78
  Capt. Robt. 78

Courtney, cont'd.
   Robt. Jr.   78,80,81
   Sarah Campbell   78
   Mrs. Sarah   80
Craig,
   A.   81
Crittenden,
   Thos. G.   62
   Zachariah   101
Crouch,
   Lawrence   20
Croxton,
   Carter   23
Crutchfield,
   Eliz   29
Culver,
   Mrs Eugene L.   20
   Mrs. Florence B.   20,21
Culp,
   Geo.   33
Curacoa   47

D

Dabney,
   Col.   36
   Benj.   76,94
   Isaac   72
   Capt. Richd.   35
   Susannah   72
Dabney's Legion   12
Dame,
   Geo. G.   65
Dartmouth,
   Lord   40
Davis,
   Anderson   65
   Mrs. Catherine   30,31
   Joshua   32
   May   30
   Pleasant   31
Day,
   Jos.   75
Dedlock (Didlake?),
   Jno.   65
Delany,
   Thos   2
Derieux,
   Peter J.   23
Deserters,   14
Deshazo,
   Ensign Larkin   61
   Martha   78
Dew,
   Thos. 21,59,61,76
Didlake (Dedlock?),
   Jno.   65
   Lt. Wm.   59,61
Diggs,
   Dudley   64
Dillard,
   John   65
   William   65
Dix,
   Gabriel   101
Dixon,
   Col.   50
Douglas,
   Thos.   63
Drabelle,
   John F.   64
Dudley,
   Ambrose   51
   Banks   9
   Geo. B.   65
   Paulin   65
   Richd.   65
   Thos.   65
   Wm.   86
Dugan,
   Wm. H.   38
Duke University   46,99

Duling,
   Achilles   96,97
Dunkirk,   96,97
Dunlop,
   L.H.   99
   Leonard Hill   99
   Sarah Thacker   99
   William   99
Dunmore,
   Lord   40,43
Dunn,
   Jno. W.
Durham,
   Ambrose   63

E

Edmondson,
   Thos.   6
Edwards,
   J.L.   23,36,37
   James T.   30
   Thos.   6
Elliott,
   Agnes   72
   Mrs. Sarah 24,25,26,27,
                         28
   Temple   72
   Wm.   24,25,26,27,85
   Wm. C.   28
Endfield P.O., King Wm.
   Co.   37
Ennis,
   Col.   36
Eubank,
   Christopher   63
   John   16,17,63
   Mrs. Katherine 16,17,
                         18
   Richd.   31,34
   Thos.   65
   Warner   64
   William   63
Evans,
   John   4,9

F

Faubous,
   Wm.   2
Faulkner,
   Capt. Thos.   64,95
Fauntleroy,
   Griffin (killed at
      Battle of Monmouth)
                         19
   Saml.   86,92
Figg,
   William C.   65
Fitzhugh,
   Wm   27
Fleet,
   Capt. Baylor   58
   Christopher B.   99
   Edwin   33
   Geo. B.   62
   John   76
   Jas. Robt.   46
   Josiah Ryland   46
   Priscilla   46
   Capt. William 46,50,
                  57,60,87
Fleet Papers,   68
"Fleetwood", K & Q Co. 28
Fleming,
   John   63,65
   Robt.   33
   Thos.   63
Fogg,
   - - -   73
   John   74

Fogg, cont'd.
   Joseph   74
   Nathaniel   65,74,75
   Thos.   65,74
Foster,
   Cosby   9
   Peter   34
   Thos.   33
Fouler,
   Patrick   33
Four Mile Creek,   35
Fox,
   Edw.   78
   Edwd. Campbell   78,79
   James   36,37,38
Franklin,
   Sampson   6
Frazer,
   Alex   63
Frazier,
   James   3,4
Frayser,
   John Jr.   10
   Wm.   9,10,11
Frazer's Ferry, 10,35,100
Froman,
   Jno.   65
Fry,
   Col. Joshua   1
Gaines,
   Benj.   59,60
   James   63
   Richd.   64
   Robt.   65
   Ro. B.24,28,30,34,37,38
Gamble,
   Col. Robt.   74
Gardner,
   Dr. Antho: 86
Garnett,
   Ensign Henry   60,61
Garrett,
   Ensign Robt.   61
Gates,
   Gen'l.   21
Gates Defeat,   21,35
Gatewood,
   Chaney   76
   William   101
Geddy's Tavern   100
Gentry,
   John   32
   Priscilla   31,32
George,
   Mrs.   82,83
Gibson,
   Col. Geo.   12,15
Gloucester Point,   36
Goodman,
   Geo.   22
Gouldman,
   Edwd.   95
Graham,
   William   41,43
Graves,
   Francis   26
Green,
   Col.   14
   George   95
"Greenbrier", K&Q Co. 82,83
Greenstreet,
   Jos.   65
Greenwood,
   Margaret   97
   Thos.   97
Gregg,
   Dr. Daniel H.   84
Gregory,
   Fendall   27
   Roger   38
   Thos.   9
   Thos. W.S.   36,38

Gresham,
    Mrs. Ann Catherine 55
    B.F.   55
    E.J.   55
    Lt. James   62
    Mrs. Maria Josaphine 55
    Lt. William   59
Griffin,
    Corbin   51
Grymes,
    Major Jno. Randolph 42,
                        44
Guthry,
    John   8
Gwathmey,
    Joseph   65,72
    Mary   72
    Capt. Temple   58

H

Hackney,
    Eliz Lee   82
    Maria Meacham   82,83
    Nancy   82
Haile,
    Thos.   66
Hall,
    Robt.   66
Hampshire Jail,   14
Harper,
    Lieut.   22
Harris,
    Henry   72
    William   71,72
Harrison,
    Col.   22,24,25
    Benj.   23
Hart,
    Claiborne   66
Harwood,
    Arch'd R.   62
    Christo: 98
    John   98
    Saml. F.   84
Haxall and Co. Richmond 54
Hay,
    Gideon   30,31,33,34
    James C.   30,31,34
    John   20,31,34
    Mrs. Priscilla   30,31,34,
                        35
    Richard   30,31,34
    Robert   30,31,34
    Sarah Ann   30,31,34
    Thomas   30,31,34
Hayes,
    Wm.   33
Hatnes,
    Thos.   79
Healy,
    Geo.   23
Heath,
    Geo.   66
Hembury,
    Osgood of London   39
Hemingway,
    John   64
Henderson,
    Jas. E.   99
    Mrs. Sarah   99
Henley,
    Rev. Saml   45
Henry,
    Charles S.   62
    Hon. Patrick   56
Hill,
    Agnes   72
    Anne   72
    Baylor   72
    Brooke   65
    C.B.   79

Hill, cont'd.
    Edward   68,69,70,72
    Frances   72
    H.B.   79
    James   48
    Jane   78
    John 51,59,60,70,71,72
    Leonard   99
    Mary   72
    Ensign Richard   61
    Robert   36,70,71,72
    Robt. B.   59,60,86,90
    Susanna   72
    William   68,69,70,71,
                        72
    William and Co.   76
Hill family possessions 69
Hill,
    Harris and Hill   71
Hilliard,
    Mary L.   26,28
    Reuben A.   27
Hillsborough, N.C., 35,37
Hillyard,
    Anne   72
    Joseph   72
Hollywood Cemetary, Richmond
                        80
Holt's Forge   16,35
Hoomes,
    Benj.   9,86,93
    Lt. Thos. C.   62
Hooper,
    William   33
Hoskins,
    Ensign Geo.   64,65
    Major John 57,58,60,86,
                89,100
    Major Robert   57,58
    Capt. Saml   58
    Capt. William   58
    Robert   86,92,98
Houtchings,
    John   27
Howard,
    Charles   25
Hudley,
    Nelson   33
Hundley,
    Charles   33
Hunter,
    R.T.M.   28

I

Innes,
    Col.   14,16

J

Jackson,
    Ambrose   63
    William   63
Jacob,
    John (Druggist of London) 53
Jarvis,
    Rachel   37,38
Jefferson,
    Thomas   45
Jeffries,
    Geo. C.   63
    Robt.   59
    Tho.   60
    Thos. M.   63
Jennings,
    Hon. Edmund   44
Jessee,
    Wm.   2
Johnson,
    Mrs. Bradley S.   46

Johnson, cont'd.
    Christopher   30
    James Jr.   48
    Capt. Philip   21
    Robt   33
    Thos.   98
Jones,
    Capt. A.C.   78
    Cha: 25
    Lt. James   59,64
    Jane Campbell   78
    Judge J.H.C.   79,84
Joseph,
    Allen   65
Judah,
    Dav: 64

K

Kelley,
    Mrs. Eliz: 28,29
    James   28,29
Kemp,
    John   4
Kenyham,
    John   9
Kidd,
    Major John 57,58,60,89
King,
    Alex   36
    Geo. H.S.   77,78
    Henry L.   17,18
Kock (Cock or Rock?),
    Wm.   32

L

la Fayette,
    the Marquis de 15,16,21
Lafonn,
    Major   95
Langborn,
    William   15,16
Lee,
    Genl. Henry   57
    Richard of London   41
Leeman,
    James   66
Lewis,
    Major   8
    Major Andrew   2
    Capt. Charles   6,8
    Capt. Josh'a   2
    Capt. Robt.   29
Lewis -
    Mrs. Sally D.   29
Lions,
    Dr.   33
    James   33
Lipscomb,
    Ambrose   32
    Ann   26
    Danl.   27
    Sarah   26
    Sterling   38
    Capt. Yancy   25
Littlepage,
    Edmund   27
    Thos.   48
Long,
    Mr. (Rev. soldier) 21
Lumpkin,
    Capt. Henry   21
    Judge John   21
    Mrs. P.T.   55
    Richardson   55
    Thos.   85
Lyne,
    Mr.   50
    Capt. Geo: 12
    Col. William   52,53

M

Madison,
  Polly   27
Major,
  John   3
Malone,
  Lony   17
"Malvern Hill",   21,35
Maneon,
  Wm.   32
Mann,
  Robt.   98
Manson,
  William   33
Mantapike Warehouse,   51,101
Marchant,
  Dr.   34
Martin,
  Thos. C. 57,76,86,88,96,
                               97
  Willis   66
Mason,
  John   19
McCandlish and Todd,   53
McCraw,
  James   52
McKenzie,
  Capt. Robt.   4,8
Meredith,
  John   66
  Sam   65
Meriwether,
  Thos.   23
Metcalf,
  Thos.   101
Milby,
  James   66
  John, Jr.   66
  Thos.   62
  Wm. B.   66
Miller,
  Simon   95
Minor,
  John   76
  Owen   66
Mitchell,
  Geo.   11
  James   62
Monmouth, Battle of   19
Monroe,
  Hon. James   86,100,101
Montague,
  Philip T.   23
  Wm.   98
M-ore,
  Andrew L.   64,66
  Richd.   63
Morgan,
  William   59,60
Morris,
  William   22,23,63
Moss,
  Thos.   38
"Moss's Neck", Caroline Co.
                       39,40,41,42
Motley,
  Edwin   68
Muhlenburg,
  Genl.   12
Muire,
  Cath: W.   83
  Mrs. Sarah Ann   82,83,
                               84
  Thacker   82,84,85
  Thos. Logan Douglass
                         82,83,84
  William   66
Munford,
  William   48

Muse,
  Alex P.   63,76
  Lawrence   75,76
Myrick,
  Robt.   36

N

Nelson,
  Genl.   16
  James   34
  Robt.   10
  Wilson Cary   35
New,
  Geo. C.   64
  James C.   63
New Kent County Records
  Committee,   20
Newcomb,
  Thos.   64,66
Newman,
  William   36
Newton,
  Col. Thos.   15
Noel,
  Cornelius   73,74
None,
  William   33
Nunn,
  Richard Q.   66

O

Oliver,
  James   33
Orrill,
  John   63

P

Pace's Chapel,   84
Page,
  Hon. John   15,16
  Mann   32
  Matt   32
Palmer,
  Roger   63
Pamunkey Indians,   48,49
Pannells,   100
Parker,
  James   33
  John   95
  Robert   95
Parsley,
  John   33
Pasley,
  John   33
Patterson,
  Philip   66
Peachey,
  Thos. G.   51
  Col. Wm.   11,12
Pearkes,
  Martin   71
Pemberton,
  John   27
  Richard   63
  Thos.   36,63
  Wilson C.   27
Pendleton,
  Mrs. Elizabeth 77,78,
                               80
  Capt. Edmund   21
  Edmund   50
  Edmund, Jr.   99
  Geo. M.   79
  John   97
  John S.   28
  Mary C.   77
  Col. Philip 57,58,86,

Pendleton, cont'd.
  Col. Philip   88,96,97
  Philip B.   62
  Robt.   78
Perry,
  John   5
Perryman,
  Philip   60
Pickett,
  Geo.   14,15
Pierce,
  Capt.   25
Pitts,
  Benj.   66
  David, Jr.   95
  Taylor   66
  Younger   95
Pollard,
  Ro. C.C. Kg. Wm. 24,26,
                       27,29,36
  Robt. Jr. C.C.KQ. 21,23
                 70,84,85,86,93,98
                              100
Pollard,
  James Otway   31
Prentis,
  Robt.   53
Prince,
  Robt.   66
Prunty,
  John   14,15
Pryor,
  Major   15
  J.   13
Purks,
  Joseph   96
Pynes,
  Clement   63

Q

Quarles,
  Capt. Harry   35,38
  Capt. John   21,26,32,35
Quarles Warehouse,   9,51

R

Radford,
  Col. Wm   48
Ragsdale,
  Drury   48
Ransolph,
  Mrs. Ariana   44
  Hon. Edmund   44
  John   44
Randolph-Macon College,   83
Rea,
  John   7
Reynolds,
  Powell   66
Rice,
  Mrs. Frances   30,31
  Richd. S.   66
  Saml.   66
Richards,
  Brecken (or Buckin?)31
  Lt. John   23,59,98
  Thomas   81
  William   81
Richardson,
  William   72
  Wm. H.   25
Richason,
  Will: 64
Richerson,
  Giles   97
Richeson,
  Col. Holt   21,36
"Richland", Caroline Co.
                       39,40,41,42

Rick,
  Fanny   33
  Richd.   33
Riddle,
  Richd.   4
Ritchie,
  James and Co.   95
Roane,
  Capt. Christopher   22
  John   10,11,63
  Hon. J.J. (?)   38
  Judge Spencer   56,63
  Thos.   27
  Thos. Jr.   60,86,90
Roberts,
  John   65
  John B.   64
Robertson,
  Isaac   68,69,72
  Lucy   68
  Rachel   68
Robinson,
  Beverley   57,60,70
  Charles   94
  John   50,51
  Needler   94
  Thos.   24,26
  William   94
Rock, (Kock or Cock?)
  Wm.   32
Rootes,
  Philip   50
Rowe,
  Anderson   66
  Francis   23,62
  Thos.   76
  Wilson   98
Roy,
  Capt. Beverly   11,86,92,
                           95
  James H.   64
Rutherfoord,
  Anna   46
  Governor John   46
  Thos.   46
  William   46
Ryland,
  Josiah   60,82,83

S

Sadler,
  Jno.   97
Sale,
  A.G.   82
Samuel,
  Gray   96,97
Satewhite,
  John   32
Satterwhite,
  Jno.   32
Saunders,
  Francis   9
  R.   28,30
  William A.   30,31
Schools,
  John   96,97
Scott,
  Anderson   86
  Francis W.   84
  John   95
Sears,
  Philip   66
  Thos.   66
Segar,
  John   60
  John, Jr.   96
  Richd.   76,96,97
Segar vs Samuel,   96
Semple,
  John W.   68,69
  Lucy   68
  Robt. B.   86,90

Sewell's Ordinary,   38
Shackleford,
  Alex   19,20,22,23
  Christopher   64
  Capt. Lyne   58,76
  Lt. Richd. T.   59,61
  Capt. Wm.   59,60
  Will T.   63
  Zachariah   61
Shepherd,
  Edw.   31
  Mrs. Eliz   83
  Faney   33
  Frances   34
  James   30,31,32,33,34,
                           35
  Mary   34
  Nancy   34
  S.   13
  William   34
Shepherd's Warehouse,   101
Skelton,
  Meriwether   98
Skyrin,
  John   36,37,38
Slaves - Hill family,   68
Slaughter,
  Stephen   66
Sloan,
  Alex: 16,17,18
Smith,
  Judge F.W.   46,81
  Capt. Gregory   12,54
  Col. Larkin   58,86,87
  James   38,46
  Robert   65,98
  Robt. Jr.   98
  Thos. G.   65
Smither,
  Gouldman   64,66
Sorrell,
  Jno.   8
Southall,
  Col. Turner   14
Southworth,
  Jno.   29
  William   29
Spearman,
  Edmund   96
Spencer,
  Hezekiah   36,37
  Minetree   20
  Ro. M.   20
  Thos. F.   23,24,62
Spiller,
  Capt.   30
  Benj.   76
Spotswood,
  Capt. Robt.   8
Stephens,
  Lieut: Col: 5
  John A.   18
Sterling,
  Maj. Genl. Lord   13
  Capt. Rhoderick   58
Stevens,
  Genl. Edw.   21
Stewart,
  Capt. Robt.   7,8
Stubbs,
  Francis F.   64
Summerson,
  John   22
Sutton,
  Francis V.   21
  Sally D.   29
  William   29

T

Tabb,
  Jno.   52

Taliaferro,
  Mrs. Eliz L.   82,83
  John   37
Taley,
  Alishua   33
  William   33
Taylor,
  Col.   36
  Edmond   66
  Saml.   75
  Hon. Wm. P.   36,37
Temple,
  Lt. Humphrey   59
  John   58,59
  Capt. Wm.   58
  William   86,93
Temple and Scott   51
Terry,
  Champion   66
Thacker,
  Sarah   99
Thomas,
  Francis   6
  George   33
  John   66
  Josiah   63
Thornton,
  Jas. R.   66
  Maria Meacham   82
Thurlow, (?),
  Benj.   27
Todd,
  Bernard   53
  Thomas W.   62
  William   51
  Will, D.C.C.   70,101
Todd's Warehouse   51,101
Toler,
  Benj.   34
Toomly,
  Peter   79
Tompkins,
  Christopher 29,30,32,68,
                     69,70,72
Trice,
  Robert   63
Trigg,
  John   7
Triplett,
  Thornton   30
Truslow (?),
  Benj.   27
Tuck,
  Henry   66
  Robert   66
Tunstall,
  Capt. Cuthbert   58
  John Orell   52
  Richard   52,53
Turner,
  Geo.   41,42
  James   51
  William D.   31
Turner's Tavern,   96

U

Upshaw,
  Edwin   54
  Gavin   23

V

Valentine,
  David   26,37
Valley Forge   19
Van Buren,
  Hon. Martin   38
Vaughan,
  John   66

W

Wacher,
   Dr. Jacob D.   63
   (There is a perfectly beautiful miniature of this old gentleman, owned by Judge and Mrs. William Fleet of "Greenmount". It was buried, along with the silver, in the garden at "Greenmount" to prevent theft by the Union troops, who took everything they could steal in this section, during the Civil War. It was damaged by dampness. The writer was fortunately able to repair it fairly well a few years ago.   B.F.
Waddill,
   Roland Acree   77
Waggener,
   Capt. Tho.   3,7,8
Wainewright,
   Robt.   71
Walden,
   John   66
   Richard   63
   William   63
Waldo,
   Hon. L.P.   30
Walker,
   Frances   72
   Capt. Humphrey 58,86, 90,91,100
Walker,
   John   82
   Robert   66
   Thomas   1,72
Waller,
   Hon. B.   53
War Vessels (Revolution), 10,11
Ware Church,   38
Waring,
   William, Jr.   95
Washington, General George, 1,7,8,19
Wathan,
   Leond.   65
Watkins,
   John   66
   Philip, Jr.   66
   Philip, Sr.   64,66
   Wm.   64,66
Watson,
   John   45
Watts,
   Danl.   62
   John   101
   Kaufmann   60
   Mrs. Polly   22,23
   Thos.   63
Webb,
   George   52
   James, Attorney, 46,47, 75,76,81,95,97,98, 99,100
   Mrs. Mary   47
   Thos.   47
Wedderburn,
   Capt. John   58,89,86
Wheely,
   Thos.   66
Whitlock,
   Mrs. Frances   27
   James   25
   James' widow   26

Whitlock, cont'd.
   William   64
   Wm. (son Jno)   66
   Wm. (son Jos)   66
Widgeon,
   Levin   66
Willeroy,
   Richard   35,36,37
Williams,
   Charles   98
   Christopher 22,23,24
   Leonard   67
   Thad   95
   Thos.   63
Willimore,
   James   3,4,7,9
Wilson,
   Benj.   3
Wingfield,
   James C.   25
Wodey,
   William   32
Wood,
   Mrs. Eliz (Campbell), 78
   James   78
   John C.   77
   William H.   77
Woodard,
   Capt.   8
Woodson,
   Major Fredk: 15
Wright,
   Edwd: 60,61
   Wm. A.   65
Wyatt,
   Henry   76
   R.B.   28
   Richd.   64
   William   63

Y

Young,
   Henry   86,91,100
   Gen'l Henry   57
Yorktown, Seige and
   Surrender   19
   After Surrender   22

* * * * *